IMAGES
of America

CLEVELAND AREA
DISASTERS

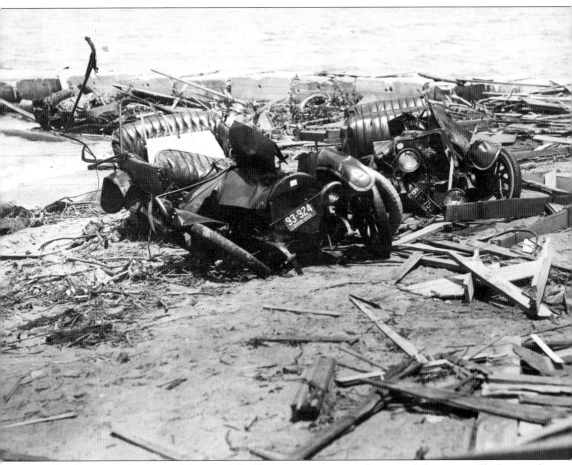

The shore near the Lorain Municipal Bathhouse was strewn with automobiles, manically dispersed there by the Lorain-Sandusky tornado on June 28, 1924. The now infamous tornado formed over Sandusky Bay. After slamming Sandusky, it briskly moved across Lake Erie and arrived ashore at the bathhouse in Lakeview Park, where it promptly disposed of eight victims as well as the bathhouse. (Courtesy of Special Collections, Michael Schwartz Library, Cleveland State University.)

ON THE COVER: Looking north on Broadway Avenue in Lorain, one sees the main drag in ruins, leaving little reminder of its prior status as a business district. Nary was a building left unscathed by the wrath of the potent 1924 storm. (Courtesy of Special Collections, Michael Schwartz Library, Cleveland State University.)

IMAGES of America
CLEVELAND AREA DISASTERS

Calvin Rydbom and Thomas Kubat

Copyright © 2013 by Calvin Rydbom and Thomas Kubat
ISBN 978-1-4671-1025-9

Published by Arcadia Publishing
Charleston, South Carolina

Printed in the United States of America

Library of Congress Control Number: 2013932732

For all general information, please contact Arcadia Publishing:
Telephone 843-853-2070
Fax 843-853-0044
E-mail sales@arcadiapublishing.com
For customer service and orders:
Toll-Free 1-888-313-2665

Visit us on the Internet at www.arcadiapublishing.com

Contents

Acknowledgments		6
Introduction		7
1.	The Early Cleveland Fire Department	9
2.	Lake(view) of Fire	17
3.	Water Above, Death Below	33
4.	104 Seconds over Lorain County	41
5.	No Building is Fireproof	53
6.	Smoke on the Water	67
7.	Death Race 1949	75
8.	The Day the Show Did Not Go On	87
9.	Streets of Fire	97
10.	The Worst Rush Hour in Cleveland History	117
Bibliography		127

Acknowledgments

We would like to express our gratitude to the people who contributed their time, support, and photographs to this book. Undertaking a project to tell the story of the worst disasters that occurred in Cleveland during the first half of the 20th century was certainly a daunting task and one that we could not have accomplished without their help.

The pictures in this book were obtained from the following organizations, and we wish to especially thank those with the organizations who made their use possible: the Cleveland Public Library, Michelle Epps and Suzie Dills (executive director) of the International Women's Air and Space Museum, Bill Barrow and Lynn Duchez Bycko of the Cleveland State University Special Collections Library, and Paul Nelson of Western Reserve Fire Museum of Cleveland.

We would also like to thank Arcadia Publishing for publishing another one of our books, specifically our editors Jill Nunn and Sandy Shalton for their expertise, guidance, and suggestions during the entire process.

Special thanks go to our colleague and friend Kieth Peppers. The chief executive officer of Pursue Posterity, Kieth helped with research, fact checking, proofreading, digitization, and additional photography along with providing ideas and a dry wit during virtually every planning session and meeting along the way.

And finally we would like to thank our family and friends who we are sure grew tired of hearing about how many people lost their lives in the Lorain tornado or the East Ohio Gas Company explosion. It probably was not easy to feign interest and smile politely, pretending to comprehend, when we could barely contain our excitement upon finding the perfect photograph. In reality, we know so many of our family and friends are probably tired of hearing us go on about fires, explosions, and tornados. Rest assured, we are now ready to go back to boring you with the obscure interests we usually bore you with.

INTRODUCTION

Disaster and tragedy frighten, fascinate, and intrigue in equal measures. We cannot help but gawk at the truly brutal wreckage of a car crash on the side of the road, the chaotic aftermath of a cyclone, or scorched debris from a blistering fire. The best and worst of humanity are often on display during catastrophes; heroism and voyeurism can describe the actions of those involved, directly and indirectly, often times in equal quantities. Most human beings have a morbid fascination with disasters, especially those that deliver an ample dose of death and destruction. My writing colleague and I are no exception to this rule. We harbor a morbid curiosity for these calamitous occurrences, in particular those that have transpired in Northeast Ohio. The focus of this volume will be disasters that transpired in and around Cleveland in the early 20th century.

The Cleveland area has been a victim of a multitude of disasters, both natural and man-made, since its founding. Some have brought shame upon the city and region, such as the 1969 Cuyahoga River fire, while others have barely registered with the general public, like the West 117th Street explosion. All the fires, collapses, storms, and crashes described in this book have inflicted substantial pain and sorrow on their victims and just as much interest in us voyeurs.

The disasters covered in this volume range from acts of unforgiving nature, such as the 1924 Lorain tornado (also known as the Lornado—coined by Thomas Kubat and Kieth Alan Peppers), to easily avoidable tragedies, such as the Cleveland Clinic fire. These horrific events destroyed property; in one instance, circus animals; and in all-too-many occasions, human life. The Ringling Bros. and Barnum & Bailey Circus fire of 1942 took the lives of 65 innocent animals, held in captivity with no chance to escape, as the torrid flames torched these helpless creatures.

Some of the most horrendous and tragic disasters to ever shake the United States have occurred in Northeast Ohio. Many have led to new legislation and guidelines being proposed and put into action to assure that such catastrophes would never take place again. The Collinwood School fire, along with the 1903 Iroquois Theatre fire in Chicago, helped bring about stricter safety procedures and new apparatuses in schools. It was not long after that horrific fire when the installation of panic bar latches was mandated for doors in schools.

As a result of the East Ohio Gas Company explosion, a number of significant safety measures were implemented. According to Neil Durbin, a spokesman for Dominion East Ohio, the gas company's most momentous safety measure following the tragedy was a shift from liquefied natural gas to a system of underground natural-gas storage.

In the aftermath of the notorious Cleveland Clinic fire, there were many improvements at hospitals on a local and national level. Chief among these improvements was the establishment of new standards for storing hazardous materials, such as X-ray film. Progress due to this disaster did not end with new regulations at hospitals; it also led to fire departments throughout Cleveland utilizing gas masks as part of their required equipment and the advocacy by the local government in the creation of an ambulance service for the city.

Lessons, however, were not always heeded from these tragic incidents. In the case of the Ringling Bros. and Barnum & Bailey Circus, it was not until after an even more horrific inferno ravaged a circus in Hartford, Connecticut, that extra measures were established to quell the possibility of another untimely tragedy. The merciless fire in Hartford sent nearly 170 souls to an early grave. After the saddest circus event to take place in the United States, Ringling Bros. and Barnum & Bailey Circus amended some of its unsafe practices, such as using a mixture of gasoline and paraffin to waterproof the canvas; this practice, now defunct, had led to the severity of the fire, as the melting paraffin fell upon the patrons below.

There are infamous tales of woe to be told through words and images in this book, and none more so than the aforementioned East Ohio Gas Company explosion. It was one of the most notorious and costly local disasters in terms of human lives, property, and money. Cost in the most valuable commodity, human life, totaled 131. The near apocalyptic devastation caused by the East Ohio Gas Company explosion, turning nearby residential neighborhoods into a hell on earth, as houses ignited from the inside out due to deadly gas leakage into the sewers and drains.

Then, there is the case of the West 117th Street explosion; the unprecedented detonation of an entire city block, most likely caused by the buildup of industrial waste and gasoline in the sanitary sewer lines. This was an event that seemingly can only have happened in the oft-ridiculed and habitually corrupt and mismanaged City of Cleveland. Miraculously this seemingly spur-of-the-moment explosion resulted in only one fatality.

In addition to the disasters I have already mentioned, we will also regale the reader with a potpourri of tales of the city's earliest fires, numerous Cuyahoga River fiascoes, as well as the inferno that nearly conquered the Cleveland Clinic. The Thompson Trophy crash and Waterworks Tunnel collapse round out the catastrophic subjects recollected.

These disasters helped to define the Cleveland area, illustrating our foibles and the shortsightedness that led to many of these regrettable calamities. The collective resilience of the residents in overcoming, reshaping, and often rebuilding their communities is where these stories shine. Often tragedy brings out the best in humanity, and there has been no shortage of compassion, charity, and heroism displayed in the wake of these most unfortunate events. Heroic feats range from schoolmarms unwaveringly ushering each and every one of their students safely out the school exits during a harrowing fire to a brilliant inventor unleashing his latest extraordinary invention in a wholly selfless display of valor when he and his brother descended into a collapsed gas-filled tunnel to retrieve survivors and departed alive. These tales of woe, loss, ineptitude, compassion, resilience, and valor will frighten and fascinate and inform you as well. Hopefully, there will be no Cleveland-area disasters in the near or distant future to rival those acknowledged in our book except for another Cleveland Browns football season—there is no cure for that annual debacle.

—Thomas Kubat

One

THE EARLY CLEVELAND FIRE DEPARTMENT

The Cleveland Fire Department (CFD) has been first on the scene to an untold number of events, which could easily be included in a book on the greatest disasters in the history of the Greater Cleveland area. Inside, and often outside its jurisdiction, the CFD presence has greatly diminished the effects of countless fires, explosions, floods, and any number of disasters.

CFD formed in 1863 to replace a volunteer fire department, which had been serving Cleveland since 1829, members of CFD, first responders in Northeast Ohio, had dangerous jobs from the very beginning.

Between 1869 and 1900, the CFD lost 20 men in the line of duty. In 1900, the CFD owned 124 pieces of horse-drawn equipment with 410 members and 154 horses to operate them. The turn of the 20th century would also see the retirement of fire chief James W. Dickinson, who served from 1880–1900, and the appointment of George A. Wallace.

Wallace joined the department in 1869 and rose through the ranks to become chief in 1901. He served as chief of the CFD until 1931, when he retired after 62 years of service. During his tenure as chief, he acquired the nickname "America's Grand Old Firefighter." Upon his retirement, the CFD had 1,100 members, and Wallace was credited with the low amount of fire losses Cleveland had suffered as opposed to other cities its size.

One of the most memorable early fires in the region destroyed Cleveland Electric Railway Company's carbarn and 72 of its cars in 1903. While destroying the barn and 72 cars was certainly costly, it claimed the lives of three firefighters in one of the worst days in CFD history. The S.S. Kresge store fire of 1908 was one of the most notorious and devastating disasters to shake the Cleveland area in the early 20th century. This tragedy occurred due to a display of fireworks being accidentally ignited, ultimately leading to a ban on the sale and use of fireworks within Cleveland limits.

Between 1900 and 1950, the CFD would suffer the loss of 29 men, seven of whom were lost in the century's first decade. During that era, it was not uncommon to see buildings advertise themselves as fireproof.

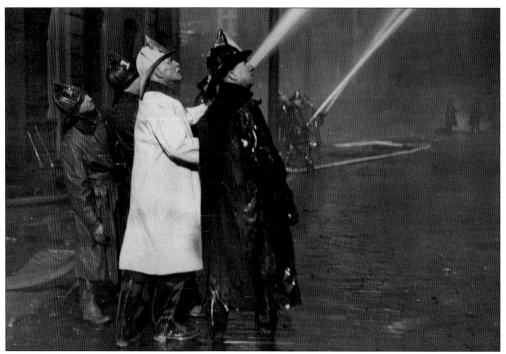

Fire chief George Wallace is seen directing his men during a fire in 1928. Starting as a second-class fireman in 1869, Wallace made captain quickly and rose through the ranks until he became fire chief in 1901. Wallace fought throughout his tenure as chief to keeps politics and cronyism out of the department; he ran it on a system based on fitness and merit. Wallace was known as an exacting commander who never asked his men to do something he would not do himself. He often risked his life entering buildings to save citizens, which, at the time, was a fairly new concept in firefighting. He was legendary among his men who would literally follow him into burning buildings. Pictured below is the fire tug *George Wallace* in 1934, three years after its namesake's retirement. (Courtesy of Special Collections, Michael Schwartz Library, Cleveland State University.)

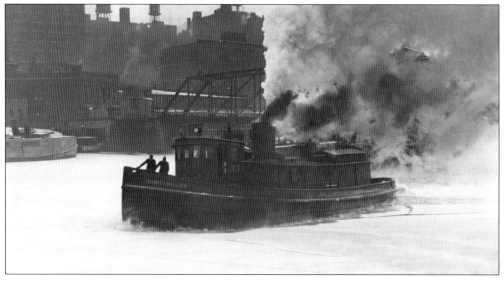

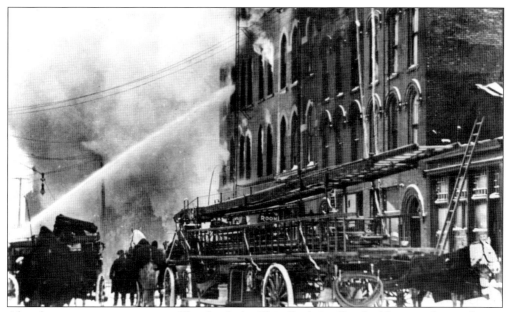

Already a premier newspaper in Cleveland, the *Plain Dealer*'s office building was lost to fire on February 2, 1908. Crowds gathered around the structure on Superior Avenue and East Sixth Street and watched as the exterior wall of the building collapsed. During the reconstruction, the *Plain Dealer* continued to be published out of an abandoned livery stable. (Courtesy of the Western Reserve Fire Museum of Cleveland.)

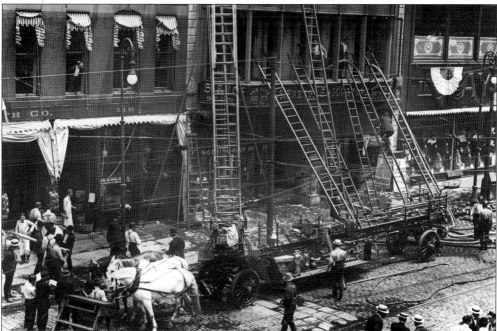

On July 3, 1908, a fireworks display at the S.S. Kresge store on Ontario Street off Public Square was set off from a still unknown accidental ignition—so not in a celebration of the Fourth of July. Almost immediately, the inflamed fireworks covered the building in a colorful, albeit deadly, blaze. (Courtesy of the Western Reserve Fire Museum of Cleveland.)

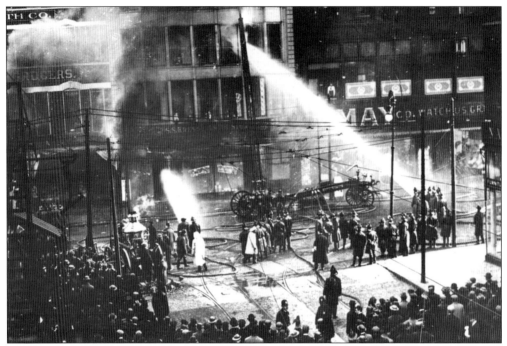

By the time the fire was over, seven had died and 25 were injured. Within 10 days, the sale and use of fireworks was illegal in Cleveland. The fireworks ban did not help the Kresge store, as it suffered a second major fire on October 29, 1909. (Courtesy of the Western Reserve Fire Museum of Cleveland.)

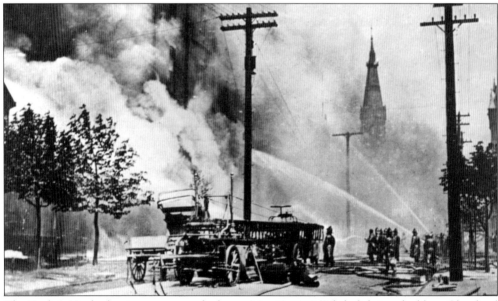

The Koch & Henke furniture store caught fire on May 12, 1910. While fighting the blaze, Cleveland fireman Herman Slee fell 60 feet but refused to go to the hospital. Tragedy struck a second time in November of that year when the almost completed new building, being constructed at the same site, collapsed and left four dead. (Courtesy of Special Collections, Michael Schwartz Library, Cleveland State University.)

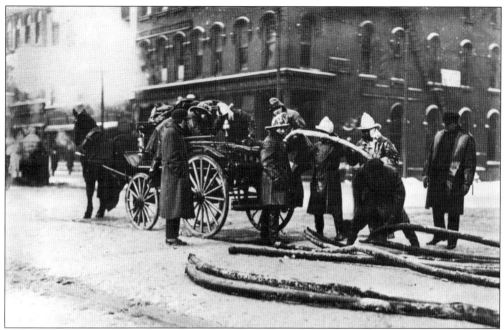

The year 1912 might have started out with this fire at the Marshall Drug Company on February 3, but it saw exciting innovations of a new era, such as the first motorized vehicle being placed into service. Horse-drawn apparatuses were soon to disappear. (Courtesy of Special Collections, Michael Schwartz Library, Cleveland State University.)

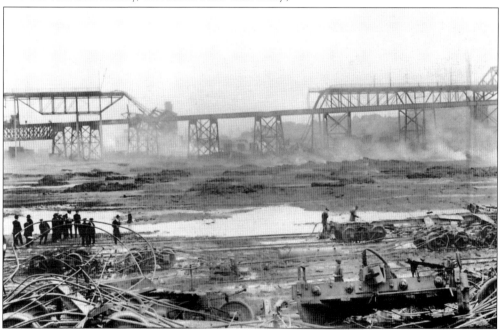

The Fisher Wilson Lumberyard fire engulfed the area near the Central Viaduct on May 25, 1914. In a very unfortunate pronouncement earlier that day, Charles Whyler, the assistant fire chief in charge of the bureau of fire prevention, boasted the city's cleanup of potential fire hazards would decrease fire loss by 50 percent. (Courtesy of the Western Reserve Fire Museum of Cleveland.)

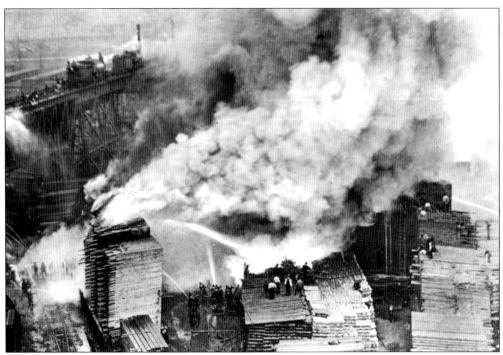

In an eerie connection to another major Cleveland fire, the Ringling Bros. and Barnum & Bailey Circus was set up in the flats the evening of the Fisher Wilson Lumberyard fire. The circus lost 25 of its 43 railroad cars that day in arguably the worst disaster the circus suffered until the 1942 Cleveland fire. (Courtesy of the Western Reserve Fire Museum of Cleveland.)

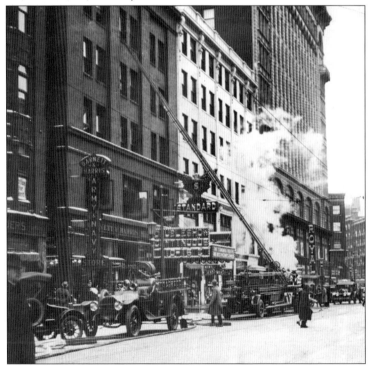

On January 11, 1925, the Cleveland Fire Department responded to this fire on Prospect Avenue. Later that year, it ordered all its stations to submit an inventory of all its "useless equipment." At that time, only two horse-drawn vehicles were part of the department's force, and by years end, there were none. (Courtesy of Special Collections, Michael Schwartz Library, Cleveland State University.)

On January 11, 1930, the Cleveland Grain Company burned to the ground at the cost of $1 million. It took 10 hours, 17 fire companies, and 2 fireboats to put out the fire, in part because the closest hydrant was 500 feet away. Cuyahoga County had bought the building earlier that day to make room for the Lorain-Central Bridge. (Courtesy of Special Collections, Michael Schwartz Library, Cleveland State University.)

The Ellington Apartments fire on June 6, 1932, is still the largest loss of life in a residential building fire in the history of Cleveland. When an explosion ripped through the six-story brick structure located on East Ninth Street and Superior Avenue, the flames consumed the entire building and took the lives of 12 of its residents. (Courtesy of Special Collections, Michael Schwartz Library, Cleveland State University.)

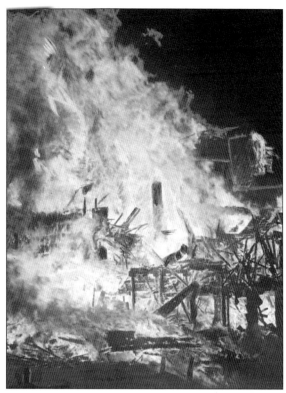

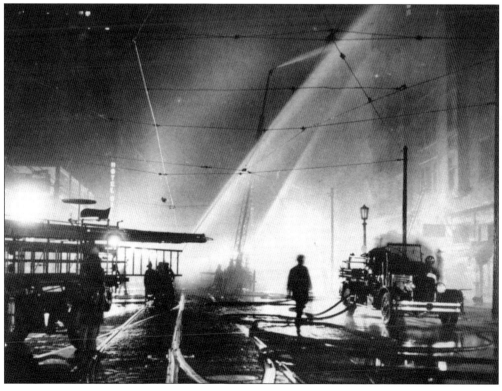

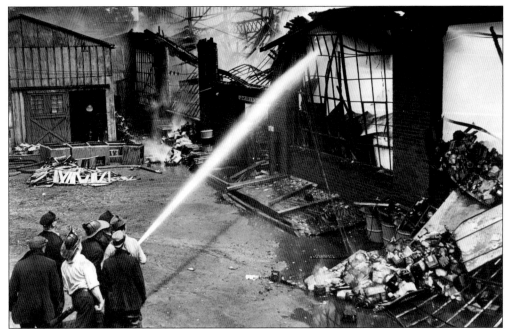

The Viking Air Conditioning plant caught fire on June 6, 1941. Just a few months before this blaze, on March 7, a general order was issued that all department members had to engage in calisthenic exercises twice each day to stay fit and trim. (Courtesy of Special Collections, Michael Schwartz Library, Cleveland State University.)

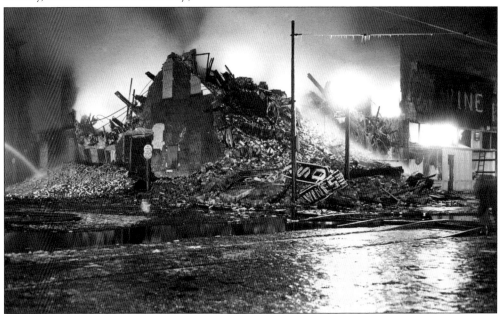

One of six fires in Cleveland's history to claim the lives of multiple firefighters was the Russo Wine Company fire on January 16, 1948. Jokes might have been made about the loss of over 250,000 gallons and 35,000 cases of wine if firefighters Paul Green and Henry Spencer had not lost their lives that day. (Courtesy of Special Collections, Michael Schwartz Library, Cleveland State University.)

Two

LAKE(VIEW) OF FIRE

In the storied and often strife-filled history of Cleveland, there may have occurred no greater tragedy than the horrific fire that devastated the Collinwood School, also known as Lakeview Elementary School, taking 175 innocent lives, including two teachers, Catherine Wyler and Grace Fisk, and one rescuer. Nearly half of the 366 enrolled students were prematurely plucked from their earthly existence.

On the morning of March 4, 1908, at approximately 9:30, a blaze was ignited in the basement of Lakeview Elementary School. For nearly four hours, parents were rendered helpless as they watched their children engulfed in flames. The blaze was finally extinguished by heroic Cleveland firefighters. The exact cause of the fire that demolished the fledgling elementary school and demoralized an entire community is unknown.

It has been well documented that the school was designed with insufficient safety measures. One long-held belief regarding Lakeview Elementary School is false, however. The double doors swung outward and not inward, as has been commonly reported. What was likely the cause of death was the lack of negotiable space between the bottom of the staircase and the nearby exit doors. In the ensuing panic, disoriented children began to stumble upon their peers, perpetuating the pile-up of pupils.

If there was a positive outcome to materialize from this tragic event, it was the introduction of new regulations and guidelines for school construction and safety that were established across the country. The tragedy helped illustrate the need for nationwide fire drills and ushered in a new era of public awareness for safety and fire prevention.

The final resting place for the innocents is Lake View Cemetery, where a memorial stands to honor all the fallen. A single grave containing the remains of 19 unidentified victims is situated beneath the memorial.

The Collinwood Memorial School was built in 1910, located adjacent to the demolished Lakeview Elementary School. It closed down in the 1970s. A memorial garden was planted at the former site of the burned down schoolhouse and still flourishes today and pays homage to the 175 victims who were relinquished of this mortal coil much too soon.

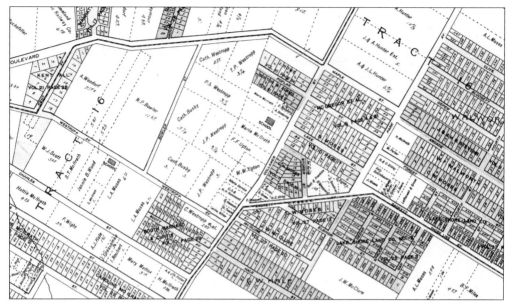

Here is a glimpse of the environs surrounding the school in 1903, just two years following its construction. At center is a small rectangle simply labeled "school"—a nondescript name for a location that would eventually conjure images of suffering children, burned corpses, and the scent of charred flesh. (Courtesy of Special Collections, Michael Schwartz Library, Cleveland State University.)

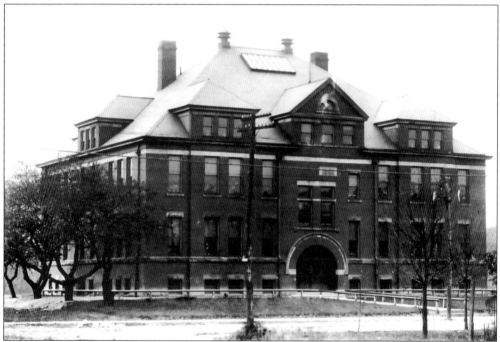

Lakeview Elementary School is pictured as it stood prior to its inferno-fueled destruction in 1908. Constructed in 1901, the school was built to accommodate the growing body of school-age children. At the base of the roof, the third-floor windows, from which many of the surviving children escaped, are visible. (Courtesy of the Western Reserve Fire Museum of Cleveland.)

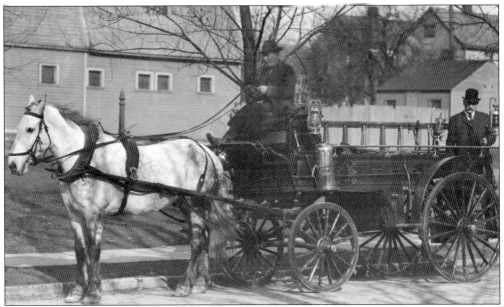

In 1908, Collinwood had not yet been annexed by the City of Cleveland. It was a diminutive, close-knit community of approximately 4,000 citizens with only a volunteer fire department to protect it from a rampaging fire. This is a Cleveland firefighter in his horse-driven engine in that same year. The Collinwood volunteers were not as well equipped as their Cleveland counterparts, and at the time of the inferno, their only team of horses was occupied with dragging a road scraper. (Courtesy of Special Collections, Michael Schwartz Library, Cleveland State University.)

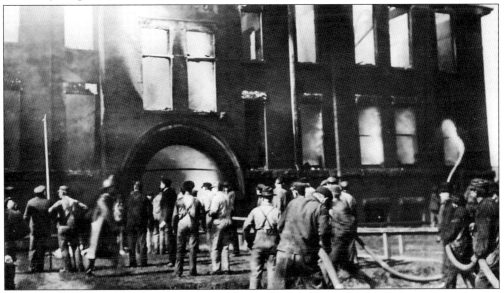

It is estimated that the volunteer firefighters took between 10 and 20 minutes to arrive at the fiery schoolhouse with only a single gas-powered engine, ladder truck, and hose company at their disposal. Cleveland firefighters, led by battalion chief Michael F. Fallon, raced to fight the fire, but news did not reach them in enough time to help avert disaster. Fallon was further delayed when his horse lost a shoe; he had to hail an automobile for an escort to the inferno. (Courtesy of the Western Reserve Fire Museum of Cleveland.)

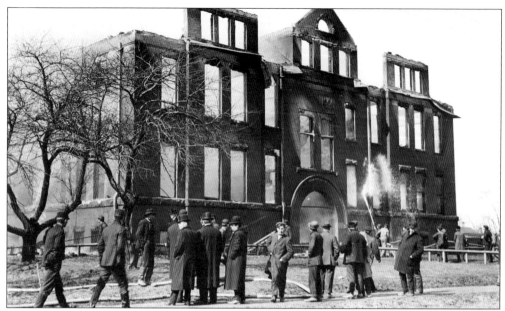

The Cleveland Fire Department (CFD) arrived around 10:30 a.m., an hour after the fire had ignited. Regarding the CFD's arrival, Fallon stated the following: "The building was doomed; nothing remained but the four walls. The fire was practically put out with the exception of some wooden partitions that were burning in basement and the ruins burning here and there." (Courtesy of the Cleveland Public Library, Photograph Collection.)

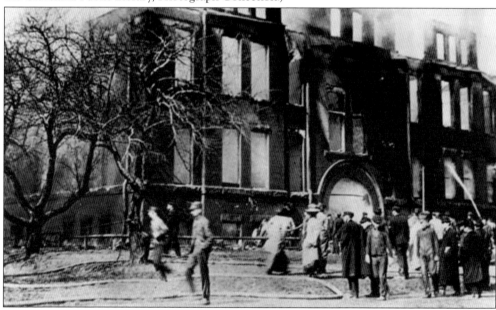

Mortified parents were helpless as they caught glimpses of their children burning alive and impotently listened to the tortured screams of their offspring. Not only did a great number of parents lose their children in such a senseless tragedy, but many of them were also witnesses to the unspeakable horror. Here, firefighters hopelessly battle the blaze as parents and neighbors offer any help they may muster. (Courtesy of Special Collections, Michael Schwartz Library, Cleveland State University.)

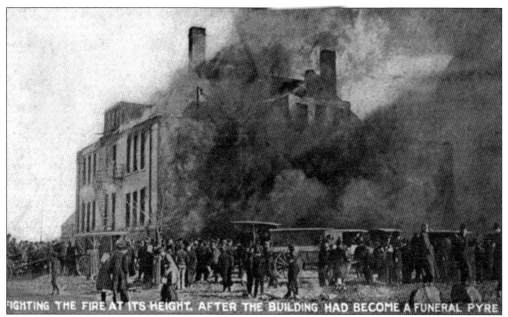

As seen here, the fire was at the height of its potency. Hope had all but evaporated by this point, as the fight to put out the fire and save the remaining schoolchildren had clearly become a lost cause. Many an onlooker were frozen in disbelief as the innocent remained entombed behind the blackened exterior. The north and west facades of the doomed school building are visible in this photograph. (Courtesy of Special Collections, Michael Schwartz Library, Cleveland State University.)

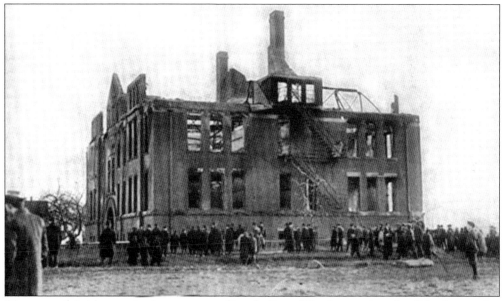

The mournful citizens voiced outrage regarding the "puny" fire force assigned to fight the massive blaze. The Collinwood Volunteer Fire Department took an enormous amount of heat for their inability to squelch the blaze; however, they did about as well as can be expected considering the limitations in personnel and equipment, which consisted of one antiquated fire engine. (Courtesy of Special Collections, Michael Schwartz Library, Cleveland State University.)

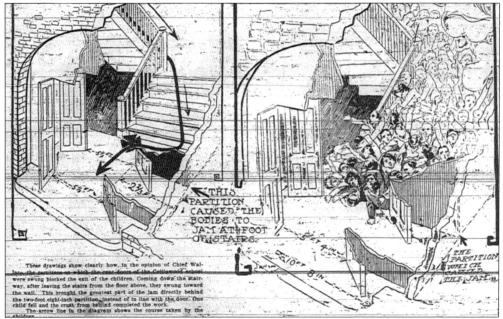

The residents of Collinwood wanted answers and accountability for the tragic event of March 4, 1908, but in the end, no one was assigned the blame. Coroner Burke declared the culprits of the disaster to be an overheated steam pipe placed too close to the wood of the joists as well as the partition built in the hall at the foot of the stairway. Though schools are inspected annually, no one deemed the partition to be dangerous until after the calamity. (Courtesy of Special Collections, Michael Schwartz Library, Cleveland State University.)

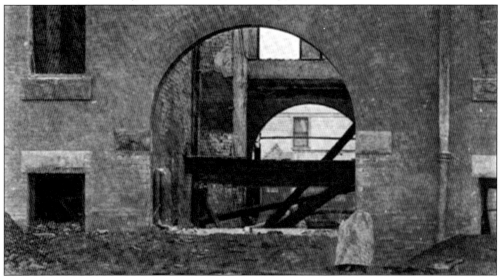

The fatal door of Lakeview Elementary School was responsible for many a student's demise. The death toll at the school could have been decreased considerably if panic bars had been installed on the doors. Coincidentally, the first model of a panic bar device was introduced in 1908 and was sold by the Vonnegut Hardware Company, a company founded by Clemens Vonnegut, the great-grandfather of celebrated novelist Kurt Vonnegut. (Courtesy of Special Collections, Michael Schwartz Library, Cleveland State University.)

This contemporary cutaway of the school's interior illustrates both the methods by which many young survivors escaped as well as the unfortunate events that elevated the number of dead. The bottleneck at the foot of the first flight of stairs created a "heap" of children, compounded by the bolted door, preventing escape. (Courtesy of Special Collections, Michael Schwartz Library, Cleveland State University.)

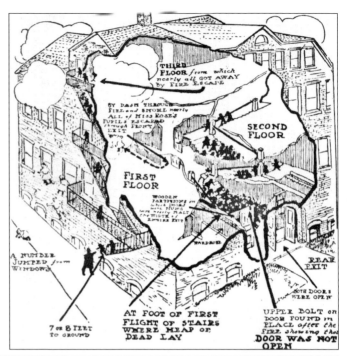

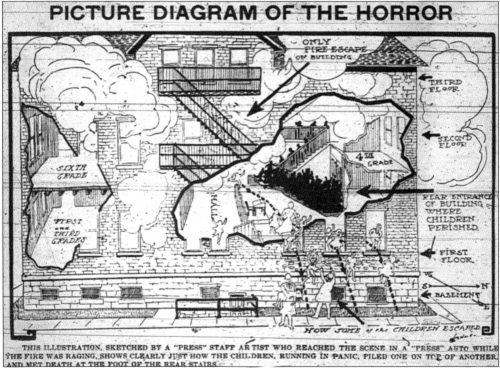

Here is another diagram sketching out the horrors, which were witnessed by those first to arrive at the scene. The fire escape descending from the third floor as well as windows, from which many jumped or were thrown, offered the best chance of escape for those trapped within. (Courtesy of Special Collections, Michael Schwartz Library, Cleveland State University.)

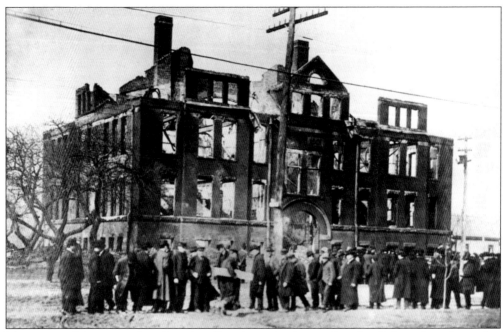

Mourners and the curious line the sidewalk and steps leading to the school's front door. Dressed in black, they take in the scene of destruction; they were free to gaze into the school's interior after the fire had died and the smoke had lifted. (Courtesy of Special Collections, Michael Schwartz Library, Cleveland State University.)

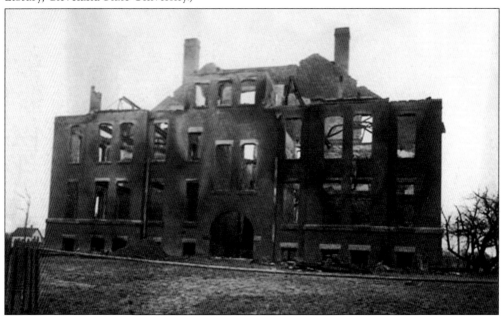

The blaze burned with such intensity that some of the bodies recovered were never identified. Its flames were so intense that steel ceiling joists melted and twisted from the extreme heat. The exterior brick facade finds little structural support as the fire, the remnants of which cloak the upper level in a veil of smoke, gutted much of the interior. (Courtesy of Special Collections, Michael Schwartz Library, Cleveland State University.)

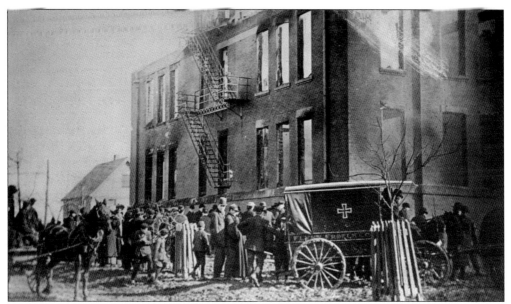

After the fire had subsided, the firefighters, under the supervision of battalion chief Fallon, attempted to shovel for bodies. Ultimately, this proved far too difficult and time consuming, thus they floated the bodies by putting a large stream of water under each of them, therefore creating pressure, which proved easy. Sorrowful family members, volunteers, and firefighters scour through the ruins searching for the ill-fated children. (Courtesy of Special Collections, Michael Schwartz Library, Cleveland State University.)

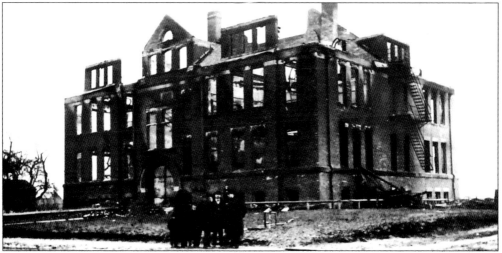

The burnt out building was inspected by public officials and fire department brass after the blaze. The aftermath seen here barely hints at the sheer horror and carnage that had occurred; the dead had been carted off in an ambulance, three at a time, and taken to the congested morgue. The corpses had been piled from the basement to six feet above the floor under the stairs. There would have been even more casualties had it not been for heroes such as Wallace W. Upton, who lived next door to the school. Upton was responsible for the rescue of 17 children plus a teacher, after which he fell to the ground from exhaustion. For his heroic deeds, Upton received a medal of honor from the Republic of France and had his name inscribed on the roll of honor in all-boys schools in that country.

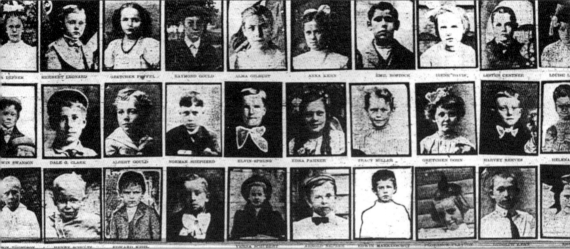

Pictured on the front page of the March 5, 1908, edition of the *Cleveland Press* are 30 of the 172 child victims of the fiery holocaust. Collinwood was a small, close-knit community. Everyone had a child who attended the school or knew a student or faculty member. The tragedy took an immense toll on every resident of the city. (Courtesy of Special Collections, Michael Schwartz Library, Cleveland State University.)

Grace Fiske was one of two teachers who perished in the fire. Fiske leapt from a first-story window with two terrified pupils clinging desperately to her skirt. She was rushed to Glenville Hospital, where she ultimately succumbed to her severe injuries. (Courtesy of Special Collections, Michael Schwartz Library, Cleveland State University.)

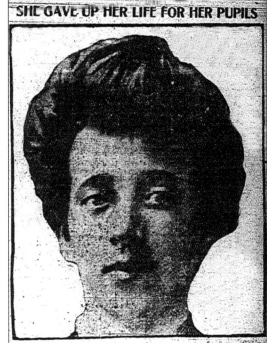

MISS GRACE FISKE, WHO WRAPPED HER LITTLE CHARGES IN HER SKIRTS TO PROTECT THEM FROM FLAMES. RESCUED BREATHING FROM THE BUILDING, SHE DIED IN FEW MOMENTS.

TEACHER WHO DIED A HEROINE'S DEATH

MISS KATHERINE WEILER,
The young teacher in the Collinwood school who gave her life in a vain attempt to save the little ones in her care.

Katherine Weiler, a beloved, albeit strict, arithmetic instructor at Lakeview Elementary School, was the other teacher who perished in the fire as she was courageously attempting to save her students. Weiler was about to scamper down a ladder to safety when she selflessly turned back to retrieve more students. She ushered frightened children out of the crush at the stairwell but was not able to save herself. Her body was found around those of students; assuredly she was attempting to guide them to safety. (Courtesy of Special Collections, Michael Schwartz Library, Cleveland State University.)

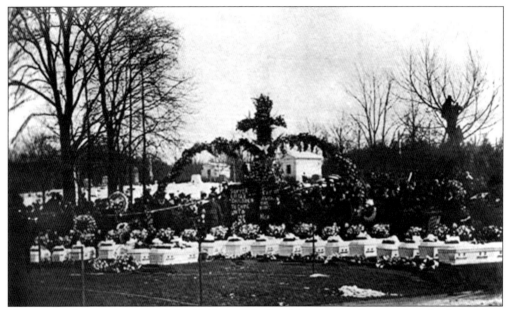

Nineteen unknown victims of the Collinwood school fire are set for burial at the Lake View Cemetery on Monday March 19, 1908. These anonymous casualties, along with the two heroic teachers, were the last victims of the fire to be buried at Lake View Cemetery. (Courtesy of Special Collections, Michael Schwartz Library, Cleveland State University.)

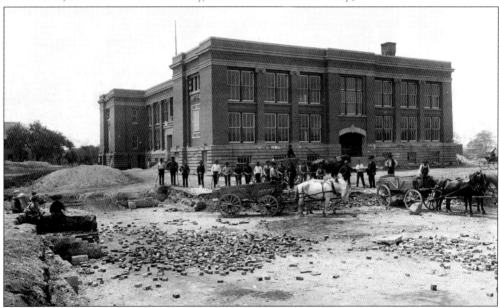

For many months prior to the fire, debate had raged regarding the annexation of Collinwood by the City of Cleveland. The citizens of Collinwood had voted in favor of the annexation, but the local government, led by Mayor Sherman, continually postponed the action. If the annexation had occurred, it is possible the tragedy may have been diminished, as the better-equipped Cleveland Fire Department with superior manpower may have subdued the inferno. Cleveland finally annexed Collinwood in 1910, which was the same year the first Memorial School, pictured here, was built. (Courtesy of Special Collections, Michael Schwartz Library, Cleveland State University.)

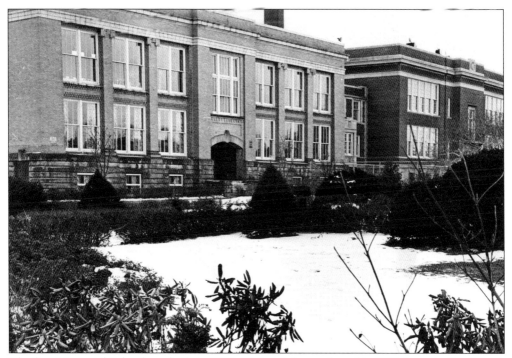

The first Memorial School was built in 1909–1910 and then enlarged in 1917. It was built adjacent to the former school. Here, Memorial School is shown in 1968, which was not long before it shut its door in the 1970s. The building was demolished in 2004, and a new school was constructed in its place. (Courtesy of Special Collections, Michael Schwartz Library, Cleveland State University.)

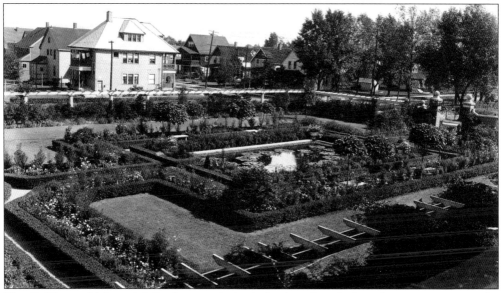

The Collinwood Memorial Garden was devised, developed, and planted to commemorate the children who lost their lives during the Lakeview Elementary School fire. Planning for the garden began as early as 1910 with construction commencing in 1916; it finally came to fruition in 1918. It resides at the site of the old school. (Courtesy of Special Collections, Michael Schwartz Library, Cleveland State University.)

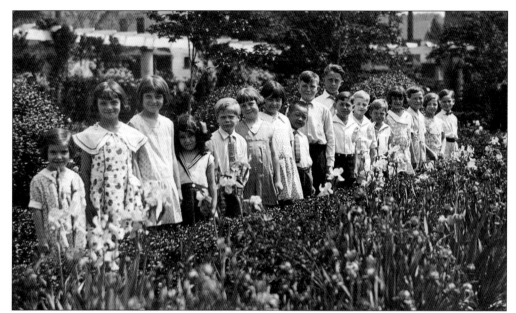

A group of children is shown at the Collinwood Memorial Garden in 1931. The Collinwood Memorial Garden was 140 feet wide and 500 feet deep, featuring a 30-by-50-foot water garden as its centerpiece. Components of the water garden included goldfish, a fountain, and, most notably, a lily pond that marked the spot where the greatest number of fatalities had occurred. (Courtesy of Special Collections, Michael Schwartz Library, Cleveland State University.)

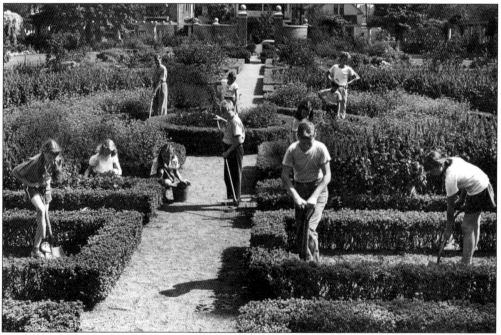

Kieth Alan Peppers wrote, "From the ground whence fire had blazed and had killed, / springs flower and hedges in the ground freshly tilled. / Children assist with the work and the duty / of keeping it vibrant, a memorial of beauty." (Courtesy of Special Collections, Michael Schwartz Library, Cleveland State University.)

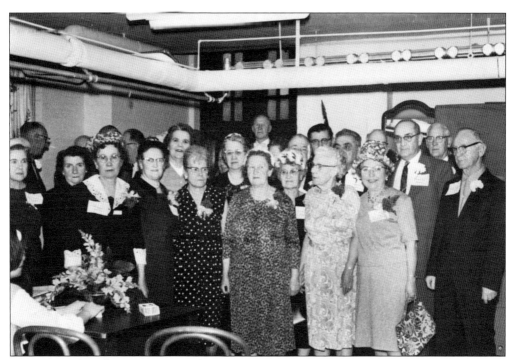

Survivors gathered for a reunion at the Memorial School on April 27, 1965. It was abundantly clear that those who perished during this pitiless fire should be mourned, but the courageous survivors should also be celebrated. The children (there were 194 students who survived), teachers, custodial workers, and family members of the dead and survivors alike should be commended for their courage, bravery, and resolve in carrying on after experiencing an unfathomable tragedy. (Courtesy of Special Collections, Michael Schwartz Library, Cleveland State University.)

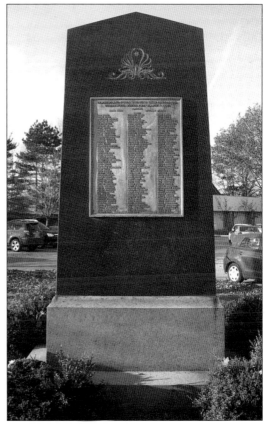

A black granite memorial stands just within the confines of Lake View Cemetery on Cleveland's east side and lists the 162 identified pupils as well as the two teachers who perished in the inferno; the memorial does not include the names of the 10 unidentifiable children or of neighbor John Kranjnak, who purportedly sacrificed his life to save those who could not save themselves. (Courtesy of Special Collections, Michael Schwartz Library, Cleveland State University.)

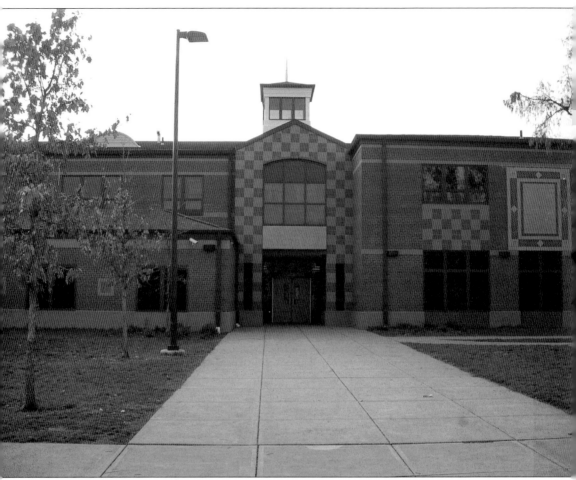

This modern looking school building resides in close proximity to the spot where the now infamous blaze occurred, resulting in the loss of 175 innocent souls. A memorial plaque sits not far from the front doors as a reminder of that tragic event. (Courtesy of Special Collections, Michael Schwartz Library, Cleveland State University.)

Three

WATER ABOVE, DEATH BELOW

The early history of Cleveland's waterworks was marred by disaster and accidental deaths. From 1898 to 1916, fifty-eight men were killed primarily due to accidents during construction of the freshwater tunnels stretching deep into Lake Erie, with the most horrific of which having occurred in the summer of 1916.

This most infamous of waterworks tunnel disasters occurred over two days, July 24–25, 1916. It was on these fateful days that 21 brave men, including 10 would-be rescuers, lost their lives. Ground zero for this industrial disaster was Crib No. 5.

Until the historic and unfortunate events of July 1916, the construction of Crib No. 5 and the adjourning tunnel connecting it with Crib No. 4 had proven to be a surprisingly safe enterprise. There had been no fatalities during the two preceding years of construction. On Monday, July 24, however, workmen digging in a 10-foot-wide tunnel hit a pocket of natural gas. A spark ignited the gas, triggering an explosion that killed 21 men. Crib workers, often referred to as sandhogs, were overcome by gas after they entered the pressurized tunnel. This calamity could have been easily avoided had the crew foreman, Harry Vokes, and the crib superintendent, John Johnston, simply paid attention to the obvious warning signs and prevented their men from entering the tunnel. An earlier incident two days prior to the disaster allowed a considerable amount of gas into the tunnel.

One positive aspect of this treacherous and avoidable disaster was the formal introduction of a lifesaving apparatus devised by Garrett Morgan. Morgan was called upon to unleash his brilliant invention, a breathing apparatus/safety hood that was a forerunner of the modern gas mask. Garrett and his brother braved the noxious tunnel to help preserve the lives of two men and recovered the bodies of four others. Garrett Morgan was a truly great Clevelander, African American inventor, and a bona-fide American hero.

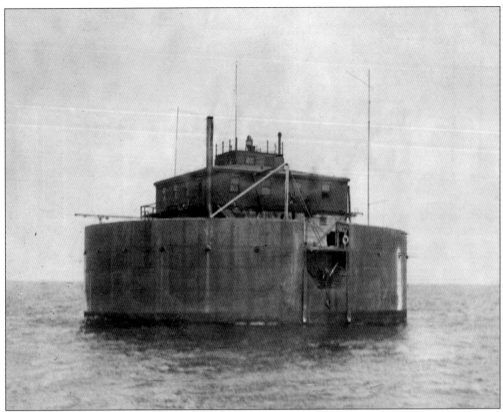

Cleveland Waterworks originated in 1856 due in part to the filthiness of Lake Erie and the Cuyahoga River. Thus, a 300-foot-long, cast-iron pipe was laid from the lake to the shore around West Fifty-eighth Street, providing the masses with a sufficient supply of drinkable water. It became clear that there was a need for an infusion of additional, uncontaminated water, and so clean water was drawn from far offshore. In order to accomplish this task, it was required that a tunnel be dug for over five miles underneath the lake bed ending in a collection point, called a "crib." (Courtesy of Special Collections, Michael Schwartz Library, Cleveland State University.)

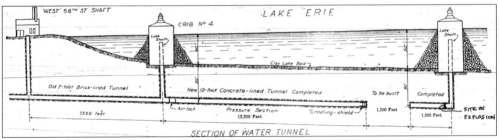

In 1914, work began on the construction of Crib No. 5, which was hauled out and sunk five miles from the shore. This diagram illustrates the subterranean tunnel's connection between Crib No. 4 and Crib No. 5, and on the far right is the spot where the explosion took place. Pockets of explosive, poisonous gas and the soft clay under Lake Erie made the work extremely dangerous and caused frequent explosions and cave-ins. (Courtesy of the Western Reserve Fire Museum.)

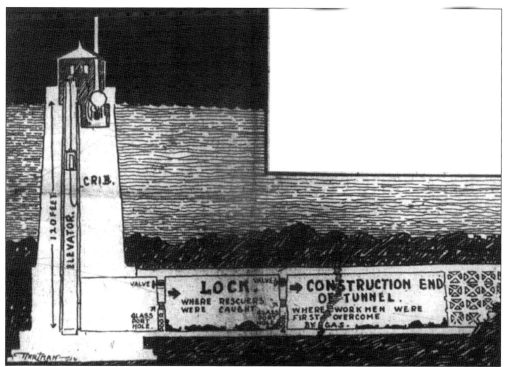

This diagram illustrates exactly where the sandhogs were overcome by poisonous gas. At 120 feet underground they were trapped in a collapsed tunnel with little hope of survival due to the negligence and mismanagement of their superiors. (Courtesy of Special Collections, Michael Schwartz Library, Cleveland State University.)

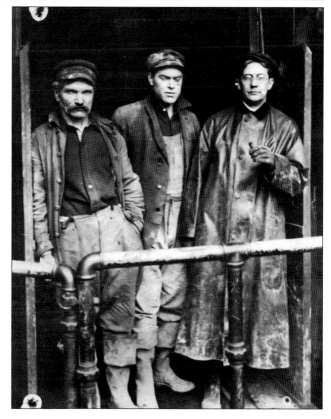

Superintendent of construction Gus H.C. Van Duzen, pictured on the far left, was no stranger to danger. In August 1901, he, along with another man, found and saved two miners who had been trapped in a wrecked waterworks mine shaft for a week. (Courtesy of Special Collections, Michael Schwartz Library, Cleveland State University.)

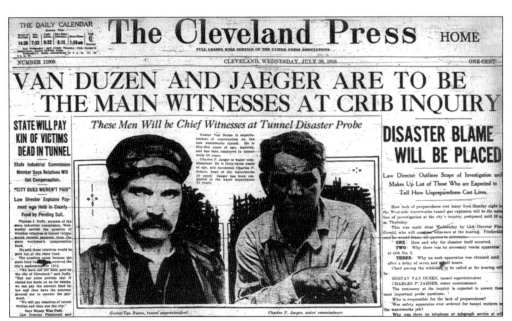

On July 26, 1916, exactly 15 years after his heroic rescue, Van Duzen was once more involved in a waterworks tragedy. He and water commissioner Charles B. Jaeger were tapped as the main witnesses to the 1916 waterworks tunnel disaster. The crib lacked a viable rescue apparatus, and none had been obtained until nearly eight hours after the catastrophe had commenced. Negligence appears to have been the main culprit. (Courtesy of Special Collections, Michael Schwartz Library, Cleveland State University.)

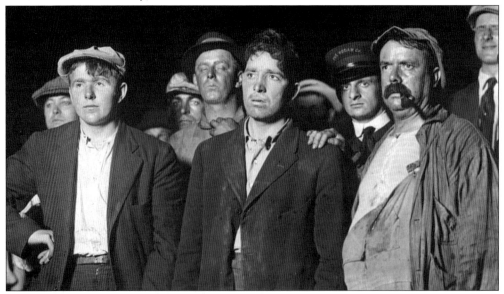

Some of the survivors of the collapsed crib are, from left to right, Mike Gallagher, Lawrence Dunn, and Mike Keough. These men and all the others should have never been ordered into the tunnel, as it was well documented that an excessive amount of gas had accumulated. This was reported to Van Duzen who had air samples taken and sent for analysis. Still men were inexplicably sent to their inevitable doom. (Courtesy of Special Collections, Michael Schwartz Library, Cleveland State University.)

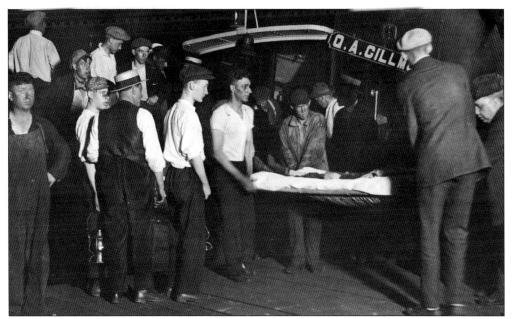

Here, another casualty is carried out of the crib; 21 men had died in all. Crib No. 5 gave up the last of the dead on August 10, 1916. The last four bodies were dug out of the mud, which had clogged up the tunnel for 278 feet. The names of the deceased were S.H. Vokes, Frank Captain, Jack Walsh, and John Patton. (Courtesy of Special Collections, Michael Schwartz Library, Cleveland State University.)

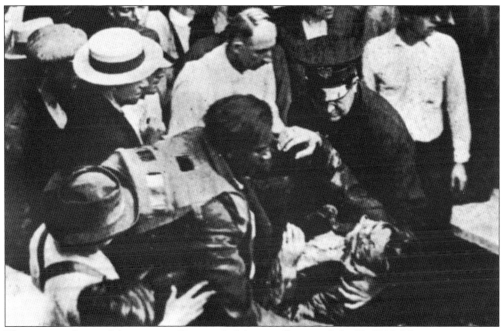

The greatest hero of this story is Garrett A. Morgan. Seen on July 25, 1916, Morgan is rescuing one of the two men he personally saved when he and three other men, equipped with his newly invented safety hoods, braved the collapsed tunnel brimming with noxious fumes. (Courtesy of Special Collections, Michael Schwartz Library, Cleveland State University.)

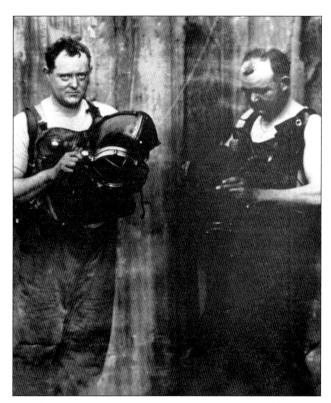

A couple of firefighters employ the safety hood created by Garrett Morgan. Morgan, his brother Frank, and a few other unidentified volunteers, possibly these firefighters, ventured down into the tunnels wearing Morgan's safety hoods for protection against the poisonous gas. (Courtesy of the Western Reserve Fire Museum, Cleveland.)

Harry Lyman Davis, a four-time mayor of Cleveland, allegedly promised Morgan the following: "The city will take care of you the rest of your days." The city reneged on this guarantee, and Morgan received no compensation for his medical bills incurred from his inhalation of poisonous fumes, nor did he receive a medal from the esteemed mayor, though a number of less heroic white men did. (Courtesy of Special Collections, Michael Schwartz Library, Cleveland State University.)

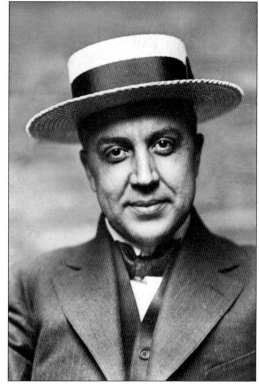

Morgan, seen here cloaked in his safety hood in 1916, demonstrated his new invention to fire departments across the United States. When in the Deep South, he would hire a white actor to portray the inventor, and he would pose as a Native American sidekick named Big Chief Mason. (Courtesy of Special Collections, Michael Schwartz Library, Cleveland State University.)

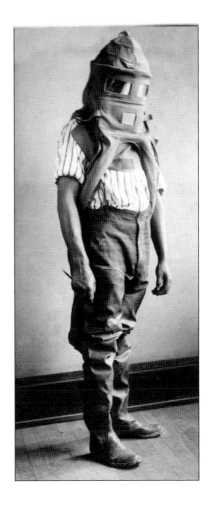

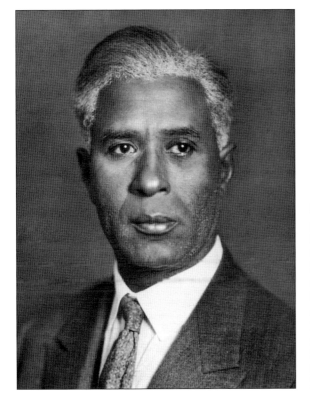

Garrett Morgan was a brilliant and prolific inventor, best known for the creation of the traffic signal and the aforementioned safety hood. In addition to his proficiency as an inventor, he also founded the *Call Newspaper*, a ground-breaking African American newspaper, in 1916. Later, the *Call* merged with the *Cleveland Post* and became the *Call and Post*. (Courtesy of Special Collections, Michael Schwartz Library, Cleveland State University.)

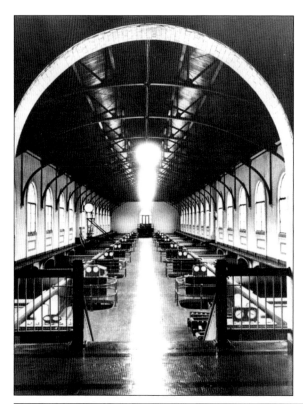

Garrett A. Morgan was posthumously honored by the City of Cleveland through the rededication of the Division Avenue Water Treatment Plant with his namesake in 1991. This photograph of the interior of the water treatment plant was taken in 1962. (Courtesy of Special Collections, Michael Schwartz Library, Cleveland State University.)

The modest final resting place of Garrett A. Morgan can be found at Lake View Cemetery. Morgan died at the age of 86 and, sadly, was not fully recognized in his lifetime by the City of Cleveland for the visionary and brilliant inventor he so obviously was. However, he was an honoree just days before his death at the Emancipation Centennial Celebration held in Chicago, Illinois, in August 1963. (Photograph by Kieth Alan Peppers.)

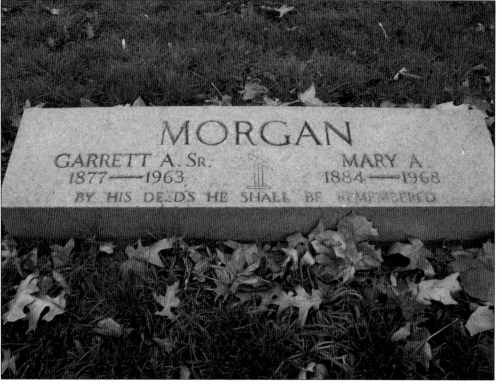

Four

104 Seconds over Lorain County

There have been hundreds of treacherous storms that have ravaged Northeast Ohio over the past 100 years, many of which were much fiercer than the 1924 Lorain tornado, but few, if any, can claim the casualties this tenacious twister chalked up. The Lorain-Sandusky tornado of 1924 selfishly stole the lives of 85 unfortunate souls, 72 of them hailing from the lone city of Lorain. The unusually large body count resulted from the tornado tearing through an urban center, an uncommon occurrence.

In a matter of 104 seconds, this catastrophic storm caused immeasurable damage to Lorain. In addition to the 72 casualties, 1,000 others were injured, and over 7,000 people were rendered homeless. Over a thousand homes were damaged, 500 of which were completely destroyed. Many churches and businesses were damaged, including the American Shipbuilding yards, the city's largest industry. The destruction was so complete that every building in the downtown business district was damaged to some degree. Fifteen of the 200 patrons attending an afternoon musical at the State Theatre were killed as a result of the tornado. Those casualties represent the largest number of fatalities caused by a tornado ever tallied in the same building in Ohio. Damage caused during this brief twister has been estimated at over $1 billion in today's funds.

Today, the business district flourishes once more. The only clue as to the inconceivable calamity that devastated the city in 1924 is an Ohio Historical Marker located at the site of the former State Theatre commemorating the victims of this natural disaster.

An interesting footnote to this tragic chapter in the history of Northeast Ohio is the contribution made by Kate Benedict Hanna Harvey, a member of one of the most distinguished Cleveland families. Harvey helped establish the Cleveland chapter of the Red Cross and was among the first to rally support for the city of Lorain after the tornado hit.

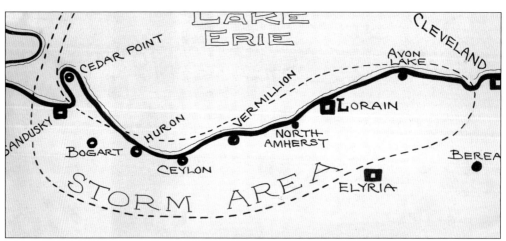

This map shows the path of terror that the Lorain-Sandusky tornado followed during its brief, albeit deadly, lifespan. The tornado formed over Sandusky Bay during the late afternoon hours of June 28, 1924, and then viciously assaulted the city of Sandusky, where it killed eight and destroyed over 100 homes and businesses. After moving east over Lake Erie for several miles, the tornado then struck Lorain. (Courtesy of Special Collections, Michael Schwartz Library, Cleveland State University.)

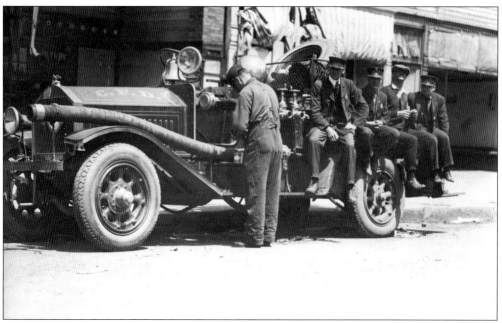

Lorain firefighters awaited the outbreak of a fire following the tornado. Because of the men's tireless dedication, bravery, and vigilant work ethic, the disaster, devastating as it was, did not destroy the city. (Courtesy of Special Collections, Michael Schwartz Library, Cleveland State University.)

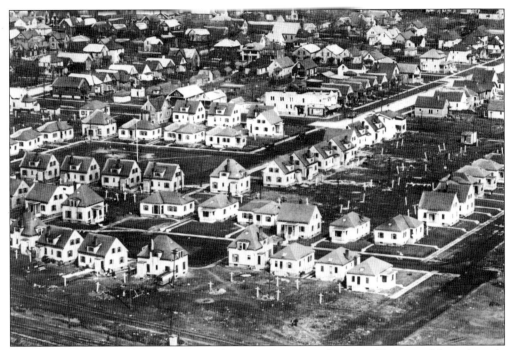

Here is an aerial view of Lorain prior to the worst disaster in the storied history of the ordinarily tranquil city. There is no sign of the horror that looms on the horizon. (Courtesy of Special Collections, Michael Schwartz Library, Cleveland State University.)

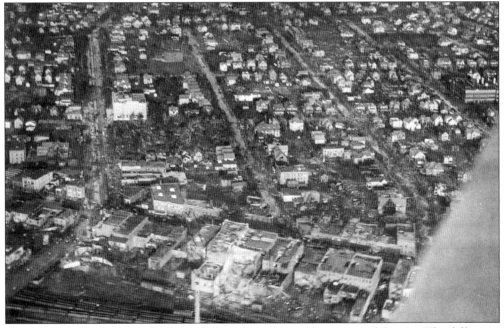

Here is an aerial view after the Lornado has ravaged a sizable portion of the city. The difference between the peaceful city populated by 40,000 relatively safe citizens prior to the catastrophe, as seen in the previous photograph, and the aftermath was immense. (Courtesy of Special Collections, Michael Schwartz Library, Cleveland State University.)

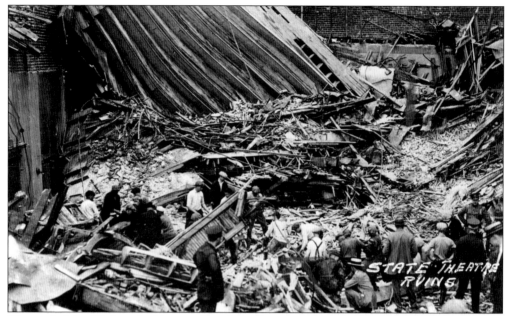

The roof of the Wickens Building on Broadway Avenue was torn off and tossed atop the nearby State Theatre. When the theater was decimated during this onslaught, 15 unfortunate souls who were merely attempting to enjoy a mid-afternoon musical were slain by the crumbling brick and mortar. This was the largest death toll ever in one Ohio building caused by a tornado. (Courtesy of the Cleveland Public Library Photograph Collection.)

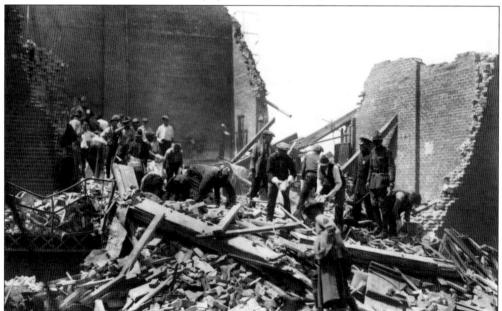

Rescue operations and cleanup of the State Theatre were arduous and physically tasking, not to mention emotionally traumatic. Here, rescue workers are removing a body from the ruins, the first of 15 such recoveries. The victims were slain when the second and third balconies, along with the roof, came crashing into the orchestra circle. (Courtesy of the Cleveland Public Library Photograph Collection.)

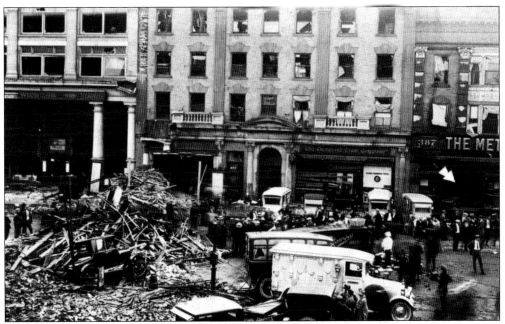

The Lornado tore through downtown Lorain, leaving very little unscathed in its wake. Police, paramedics, and firemen arrived to keep the peace and dig through the debris to rescue survivors and unearth the departed. (Courtesy of Special Collections, Michael Schwartz Library, Cleveland State University.)

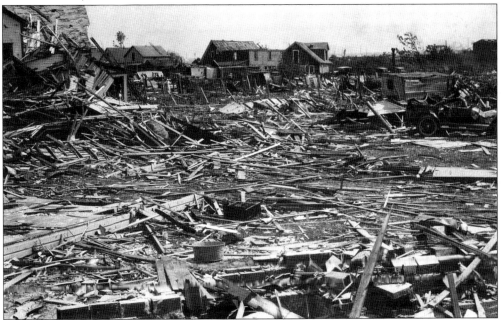

Written on the back of this photograph was as follows: "The Colorado Street District was reduced to matchsticks as the entire district took the brunt of the storm." Here, nothing remains of an entire neighborhood—a similar scene played out in all too many neighborhoods throughout Lorain and Sandusky. (Courtesy of Special Collections, Michael Schwartz Library, Cleveland State University.)

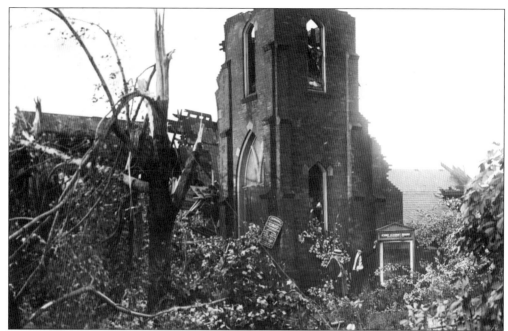

Emmanuel Evangelical Church, pictured here, suffered extensive cosmetic damage during the Lornado. Many other churches suffered harsher fates, including the First Congressional Church at the corner of Washington Avenue and Fourth Street, which was toppled over by the ferocious winds. (Courtesy of Special Collections, Michael Schwartz Library, Cleveland State University.)

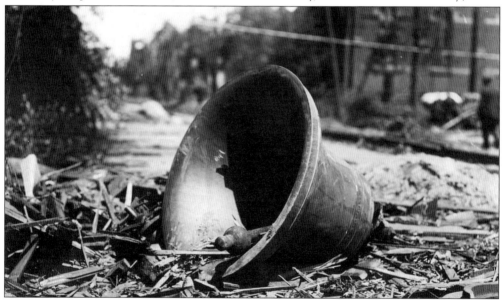

Scant physical features of St. Mary's Catholic Church remained intact after the tornado swept through downtown Lorain. The bell that had merrily rung so often to summon churchgoers and schoolchildren alike was scarred, battered, and torn from its lofty height. The church was located at Reid Avenue and Eighth Street. Subsequently, the church was rebuilt, this time with stone instead of brick. (Courtesy of Special Collections, Michael Schwartz Library, Cleveland State University.)

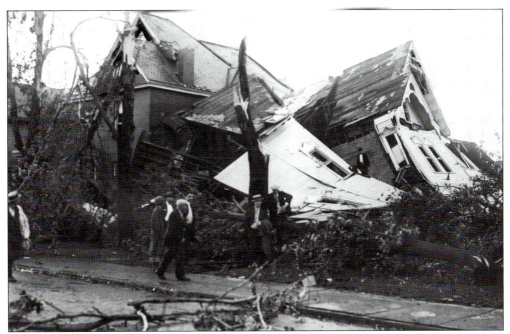

Here, the Thompson house can be seen in shambles, just one of a thousand homes that were damaged or destroyed by the Lornado. This tumultuous twister rendered approximately 7,000 residents homeless. (Courtesy of Special Collections, Michael Schwartz Library, Cleveland State University.)

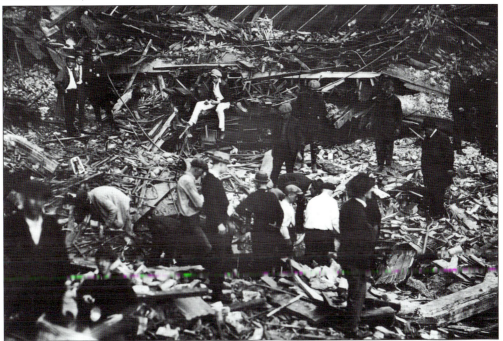

Here, befuddled citizens assess the damage after the tornado. So complete was the destruction that the streets of Lorain could pass for those of London during World War II. (Courtesy of Special Collections, Michael Schwartz Library, Cleveland State University.)

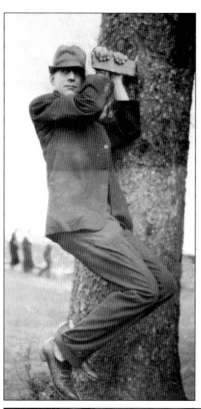

An unidentified man hangs onto a wooden peg wedged deep in a tree trunk. To be lodged so deeply into the tree, the wooden projectile must have been hurled at a speed surpassing 100 miles per hour by the fierce tornado winds. (Courtesy of Special Collections, Michael Schwartz Library, Cleveland State University.)

The resilient, industrious residents would not let a trifling obstacle, such as a catastrophic tornado, stand in the way of good old-fashioned American commerce. Here, a Lorain citizen can be seen dispersing malted beverages for a fee despite the absence of a four-walled store. (Courtesy of Special Collections, Michael Schwartz Library, Cleveland State University.)

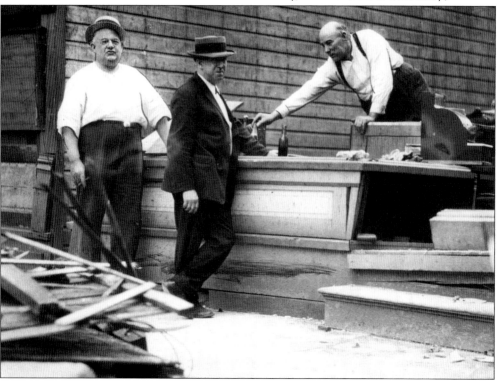

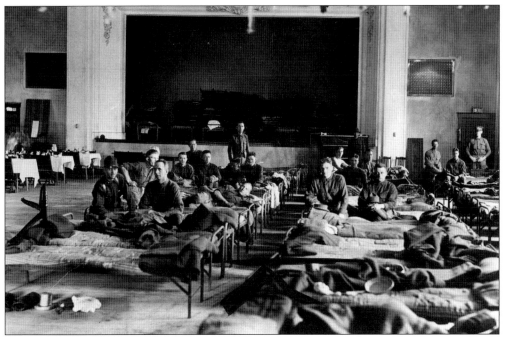

Members of Battery B, Lakewood, Ohio, were stationed at Antlers Hotel located on West Erie Avenue. The servicemen partook in much-needed rest in the Billet de Lux Ballroom after a long day of exhuming bodies and assisting in the massive cleanup project. The hotel was officially registered as a Historic Ohio place in 1982. (Courtesy of Special Collections, Michael Schwartz Library, Cleveland State University.)

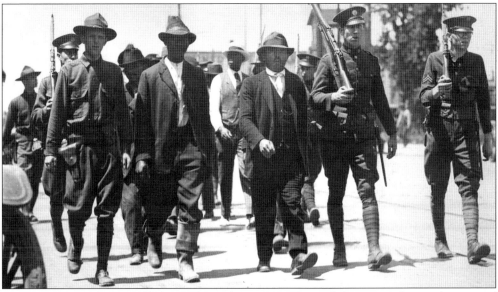

Military personnel were called in to keep the peace and patrol the streets during this time of unrest. The Ohio National Guard and Army and Naval Reserves were called in to help with the cleanup and to keep potential looters and other disreputable characters out of the city in hopes of restoring some semblance of order. (Courtesy of Special Collections, Michael Schwartz Library, Cleveland State University.)

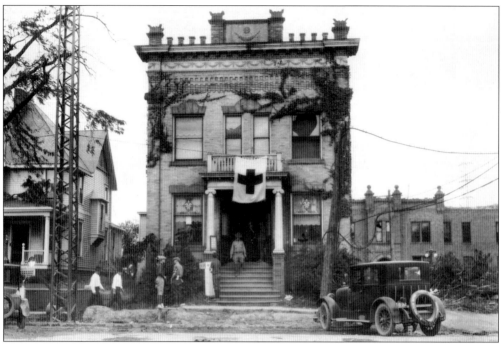

The Christian Science Church on Erie Avenue served as the headquarters for the Red Cross. Nurses were dispatched from the church to locations throughout the city, providing medical care and compassion to the displaced masses. (Courtesy of Special Collections, Michael Schwartz Library, Cleveland State University.)

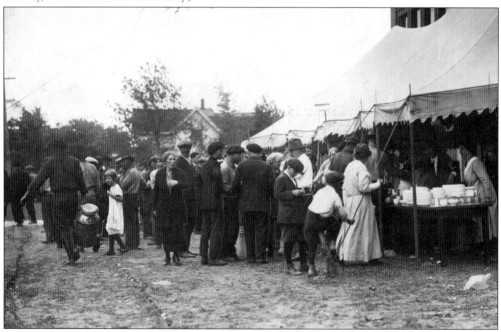

A Red Cross soup tent was stationed in front of Lorain High School. The selfless volunteers fed hundreds of hungry people. Sandwiches and coffee were served to all the needy souls. (Courtesy of Special Collections, Michael Schwartz Library, Cleveland State University.)

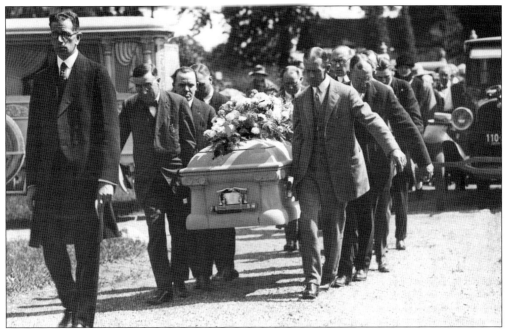

Pallbearers embark on the grim march to the grave where they will sorrowfully lower another dearly departed victim of the Lorain-Sandusky tornado into their eternal resting place. Eighty-five people were slain during the storm, although some contemporary accounts list it as 82 dead. (Courtesy of Special Collections, Michael Schwartz Library, Cleveland State University.)

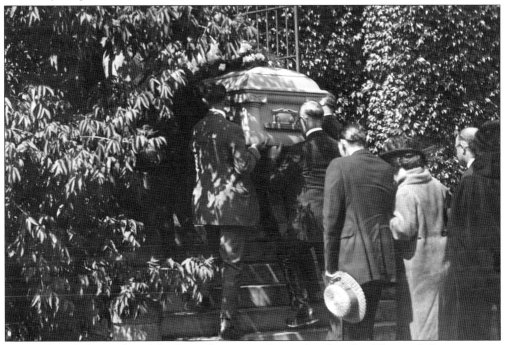

An unidentified casualty of the Lornado is carried into the chapel at Elmwood Cemetery in a scene that was all too familiar in the days immediately following the fierce twister. (Courtesy of Special Collections, Michael Schwartz Library, Cleveland State University.)

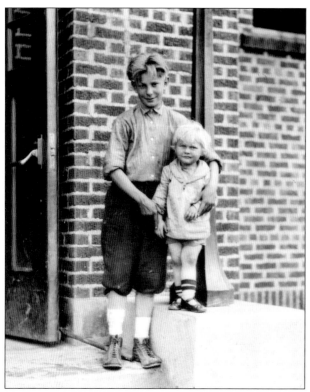

Pictured here are innocent Olga and her brother, rendered orphans by the unforgiving storm as their mother was taken from them. Numerous children were permanently separated from their parents due to this dreadful disaster. (Courtesy of Special Collections, Michael Schwartz Library, Cleveland State University.)

Here is Broadway Avenue today. The main drag is a vital business district once more, peppered with antique stores, law offices, eateries, bars, clubs, banks, government buildings, and the largest one-floor movie theater in Ohio. (Photograph by Kieth Alan Peppers.)

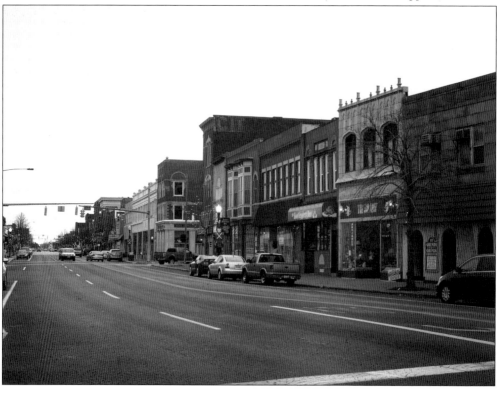

Five

NO BUILDING IS FIREPROOF

Four Cleveland physicians founded the Cleveland Clinic in February 1921. Three of the founders, George Washington Crile, Frank Bunts, and William Lower, were surgeons who had worked together in the Lakeside Medical Unit in France during World War I.

Returning to Cleveland at the war's end, their goal was to establish a hospital/medical center using principles of group practice, an idea relatively new to medicine at the time. They invited an internist, John Phillips, to join them.

The clinic grew quickly and was already internationally known by the late 1920s. Located on East Ninety-third Street on the south side of Euclid Avenue, the Cleveland Clinic of 1929 was only a fraction of its size today. When the Cleveland Clinic fire occurred, there were only three structures—a 184-bed hospital, a laboratory, and a main building, which housed administration and the offices of physicians working at the clinic.

On May 15, 1929, the main building ceased, for a time, being a place of healing when a fire starting in its basement left 123 people, including one the clinic's founders, Dr. Phillips, dead. The culprit was less the fire that burned through the building and more the gas, which resulted from a smaller fire that started in the X-ray storage room in the basement of the clinic.

The building itself, a four-story structure of reinforced concrete and brick, was considered fireproof. But as a National Fire Protection Association report concluded just two weeks after the fire, "this fire furnishes further proof that no building is truly 'fireproof.' Fire-resistive construction is of utmost value, but the value of fire-resistive building materials may be largely negative by improper interior arrangement."

Several investigations were conducted into the fire, most exonerating the Cleveland Clinic of blame. Still, it is difficult to overlook the number of American Hospital Association guidelines the clinic had ignored, not the least being the storage of X-rays in wooden cabinets instead of metal tubes.

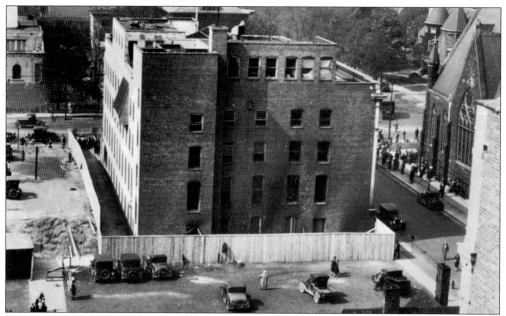

About 250 medical staff, administrative workers, and patients were in the main four-story brick building of the Cleveland Clinic when a cloud of yellowish smoke was reported in a basement storage room. The first responding fireman found nitrocellulose from X-ray plates burning in the storage room. Before it was over, half the people in the building had lost their lives. (Courtesy of Special Collections, Michael Schwartz Library, Cleveland State University.)

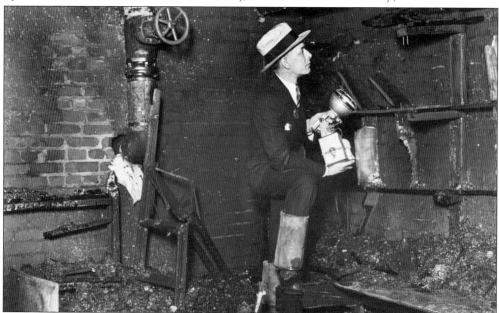

Here, a fire investigator documents the room that had contained 70,000 X-ray sheets, equal to 4,200 pounds of film, with each pound capable of producing three to six cubic feet of the deadly yellow gas the firefighters found when they arrived on the scene. The X-rays were not stored per American Hospital Association guidelines, instead they were simply placed in open wooden racks. (Courtesy of Special Collections, Michael Schwartz Library, Cleveland State University.)

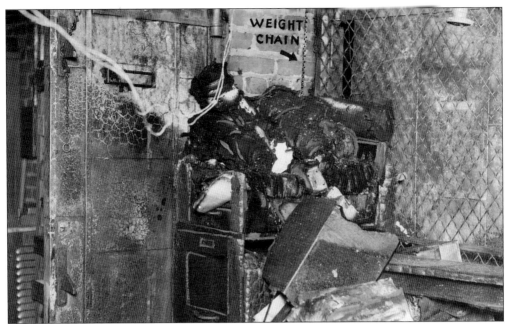

What actually occurred in the storage room was a matter of contention in the weeks and months after the fire. A number of witnesses claimed in the weeks before the fire that a 100-watt light bulb appeared, attached to an eight-foot extension cord and hung over a big spike near the film cabinets—a claim the chief custodian of the clinic vehemently denied. Another theory, seemingly pushed forth by the clinic itself, was an outside worker called in to repair the leaking steam pipe had been smoking in the X-ray room. X-rays had also supposedly been stacked on filing cabinets to avoid being damaged by the leaking steam pipe. Regardless of the actual cause, as early as May 1925, city fire wardens had ordered the clinic to keep the X-rays in metal containers and to not allow smoking in the film area. (Courtesy of Special Collections, Michael Schwartz Library, Cleveland State University.)

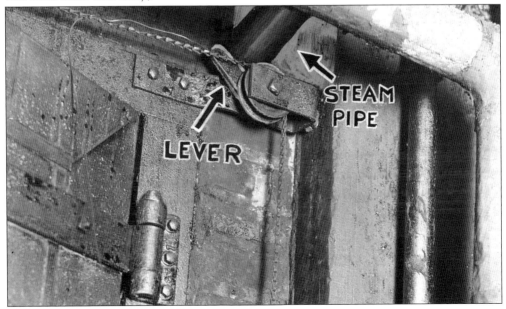

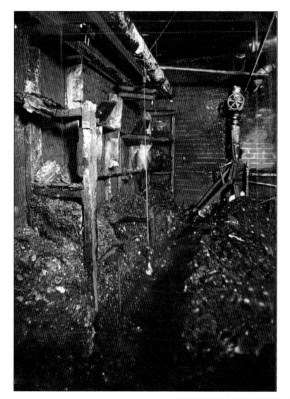

Later inspections by the city fire warden recorded that the clinic had ignored the order to move the X-ray films into metal cases. A report by the National Fire Protection Association, which was much harsher on the clinic and Cleveland itself than any report done locally, stated, "It is inconceivable that the conditions responsible for the Cleveland hospital disaster could have been permitted to exist even for a singe day had the management or the inspection authorities appreciated the hazard." The report further pointed out the clinic was still using the older and significantly more dangerous X-ray film instead of the new acetate-based Kodak safety film introduced five years earlier, which had "no more hazard than paper or cardboard." (Both, courtesy of Special Collections, Michael Schwartz Library, Cleveland State University.)

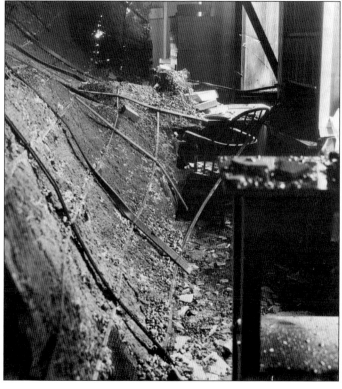

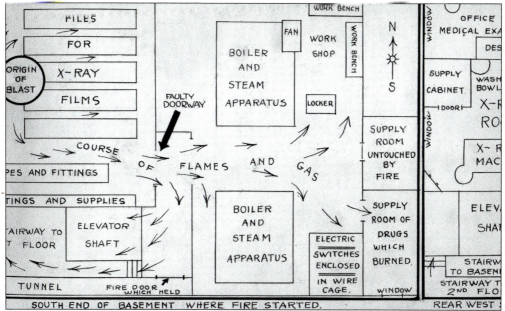

Shortly after 11:00 a.m. Buffery Boggs, an employee of W.R. Rhoton who had been called in to repair the leaking steam pipe, yelled to a clinic maintenance worker to bring fire extinguishers as a fire had started in the room he was working in, pictured in the top left hand corner on the first diagram. His later testimony stated he emptied the entire extinguisher into the fire and smoke with little or no result. He quickly found himself overcome with smoke, and, while trying to crawl out, he was propelled across the room and out of the door by the first explosion that struck at 11:25 a.m. Most experts agree many of the victims were either dead or near death shortly after this point as the gas had travelled, as seen in both diagrams, throughout the building by then. (Both, courtesy of Special Collections, Michael Schwartz Library, Cleveland State University.)

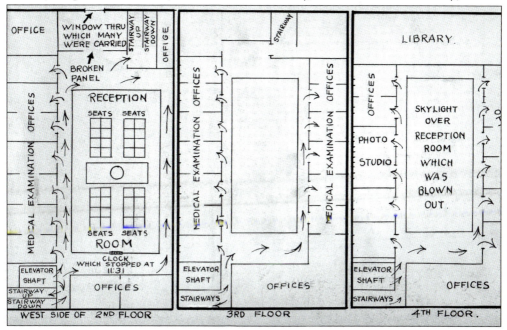

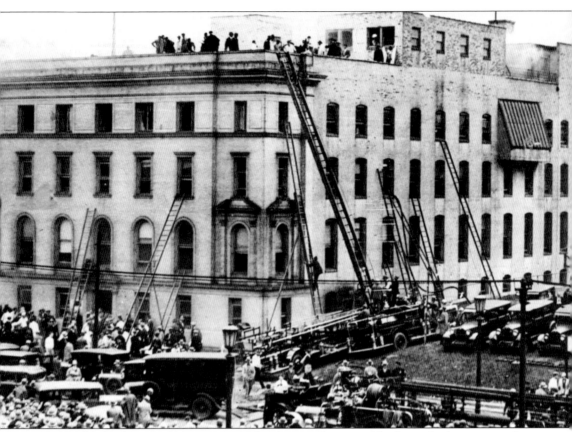

The Cleveland Fire Department received its first notification of the fire and subsequent explosion at 11:30 a.m. Responding quickly, they found entrance into the building nearly impossible to navigate, as all the upper floors were full of toxic smoke. A large concentration of smoke from the fire and fumes from the X-rays drove the firefighters away from the front stair landing when they tried to gain access to the building. Fire investigators later established fires were burning through the film room, rear elevator, and stairwell with a half a dozen smaller fires throughout the building. Still, it was the gas that presented the greatest threat. As firefighters prepared for another attempt to enter the building, a second explosion occurred. The explosion blew out the building's skylight and many windows, which allowed the firefighters to see victims at windows that had been previously hidden by smoke. Immediately, the CFD's new 85-foot motorized ladder was utilized and firefighters entered the building through the roof. (Courtesy of Special Collections, Michael Schwartz Library, Cleveland State University.)

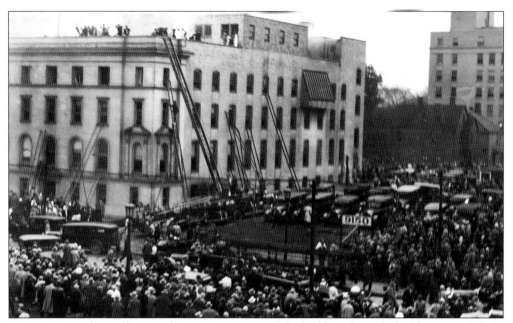

Firemen Howard McAllister and Peter Rogers entered the building through the blown-out skylight and into the still gas-filled interior court. They quickly began removing victims, some piled four high, from where they had succumbed to the gasses. They took 15 victims to the roof, although many were already dead. (Courtesy of Special Collections, Michael Schwartz Library, Cleveland State University.)

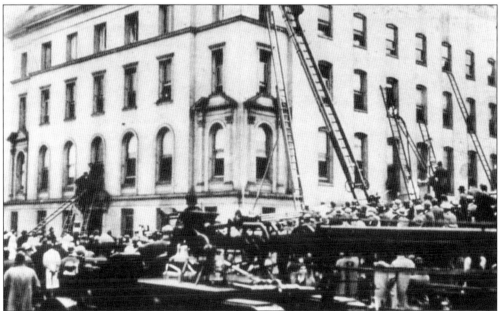

Virtually every fire unit on the east side of Cleveland responded to the scene. The fire was, for the most part, over by 1:15 p.m. with most of the victims already removed to the county morgue. Unfortunately, the county morgue, unequipped to receive well over 100 bodies, was forced to lay them out on the floor to allow family, friends, and coworkers the opportunity to identify them. (Courtesy of the Western Reserve Fire Museum of Cleveland.)

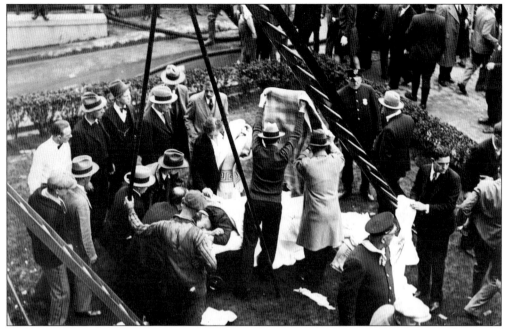

Luckily for those who did survive that day, the Cleveland Fire Department was assisted by some volunteers. A.W. Johnson and Roy Miller, utilizing 40-foot ladders for sign painting just west of the clinic, joined the rescue attempt at soon as the first blast occurred. (Courtesy of Special Collections, Michael Schwartz Library, Cleveland State University.)

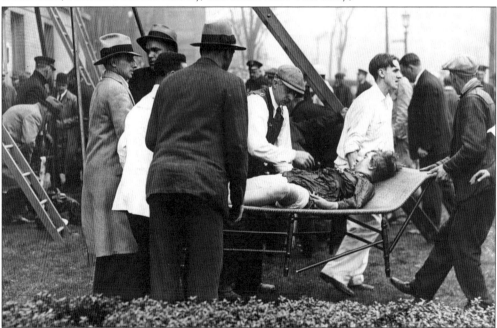

The two sign painters were quickly joined by three other men, Frank Salvini and Bruce Griffith, from local car dealership, and Walter Jackson. The five men quickly placed the ladders at the second-story windows and began to carry the injured and often hysterical victims down to safety. (Courtesy of Special Collections, Michael Schwartz Library, Cleveland State University.)

Several witnesses credited Walter Jackson with going above and beyond that of simply coming to the victims' aid. Reportedly, he carried two people at a time down the ladders during his rescue trips and held the ladders steady in the face of heat and gases from the building that virtually no one else could tolerate. (Courtesy of Special Collections, Michael Schwartz Library, Cleveland State University.)

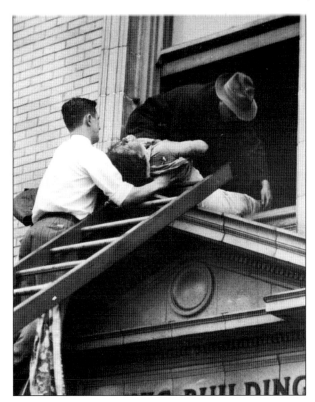

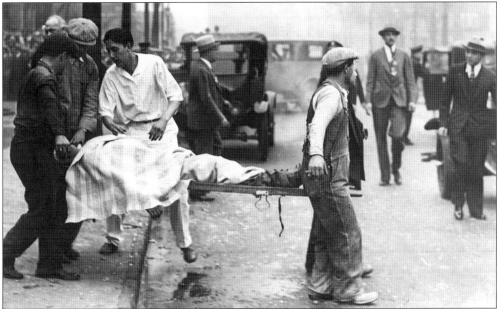

Cleveland patrolman Ernest Staab made several rescue attempts into the clinic, removing 21 bodies before he finally collapsed. He suffered from fainting spells for months after the ordeal, which considering some reference materials on the fire list him among the deceased, does not sound so bad. Staab spent another 25 years as Cleveland policeman before retiring in 1954. (Courtesy of Special Collections, Michael Schwartz Library, Cleveland State University.)

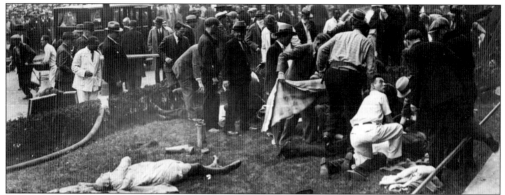

A group of students from the Wilcox Commercial School on Euclid Avenue also entered the building, against the orders of fireman, and began carrying victims outside where doctors and nurses who had escaped the carnage were administering medical care. Fourteen members of the medical staff perished that day, all reportedly while trying to save patients and coworkers. (Courtesy of Special Collections, Michael Schwartz Library, Cleveland State University.)

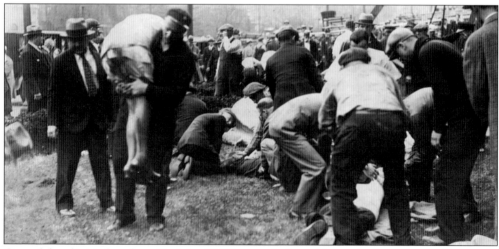

One of the clinic's founders, Dr. John Phillips, worked outside on the lawn caring for victims along with the rest of the surviving staff. Unfortunately, that evening, he collapsed and died in his apartment, despite efforts by another founder of the clinic to save him. (Courtesy of Special Collections, Michael Schwartz Library, Cleveland State University.)

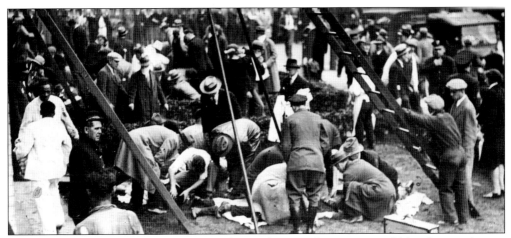

Some heroes of the clinic fire are names lost to history. One witness told local press about a young man who, while standing beside him, decided to enter the building to pull out victims after recognizing the dangerous gas. After making it back outside with the body of one victim, he turned and reentered the building. (Courtesy of Special Collections, Michael Schwartz Library, Cleveland State University.)

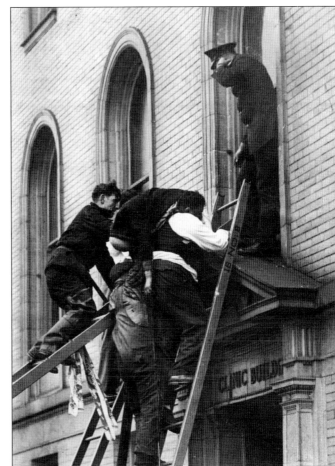

Unfortunately, so many of the victims retrieved from the building while the fire still raged were dead before the medical staff on the lawn could tend to them. Many of the 125 who died that day probably succumbed without realizing what was actually occurring. (Courtesy of Special Collections, Michael Schwartz Library, Cleveland State University.)

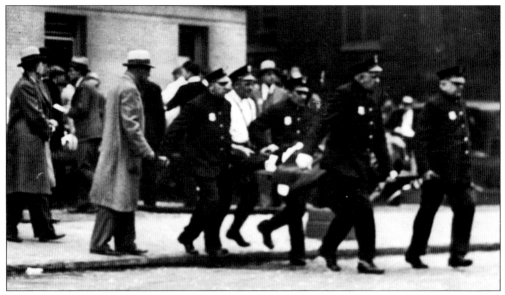

Many, though, were not as lucky. Rescuers found stacks of bodies piled up in staircases, where they had desperately tried to exit the building. The gas, a mixture of carbon monoxide and acidic nitrogen, was extremely deadly, and victims were found bleeding from their eyes and nose as their skin turned yellow, blue, and green. (Courtesy of Special Collections, Michael Schwartz Library, Cleveland State University.)

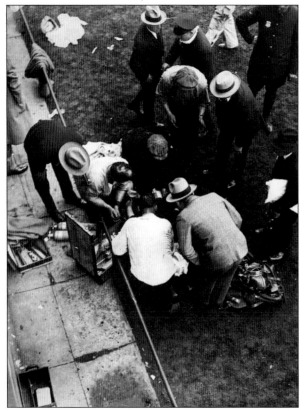

Sadly, it seems many of the victims made the unfortunate choice to attempt to exit via the staircases, which was where some of the worst fires were taking place. Later investigations concluded their safest options would have been to stay in the outside rooms and wait for rescue. (Courtesy of Special Collections, Michael Schwartz Library, Cleveland State University.)

Dr. H.L. Rockwood (left), head of the City of Cleveland's investigating commission, and Thomas Martinee (right), deputy state fire marshal, investigate the cause of the fire. Nobody or no entity was ever legally charged negligence in the clinic fire. However, some local media did point out, in their eyes, witnesses for the clinic seemingly lied during testimony about conditions in the X-ray room. (Courtesy of Special Collections, Michael Schwartz Library, Cleveland State University.)

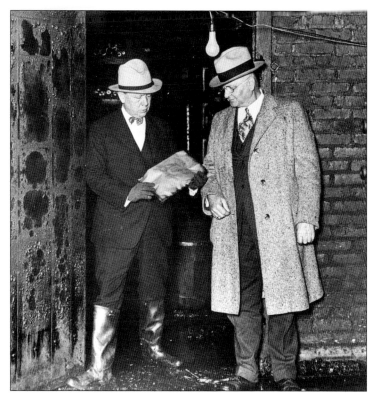

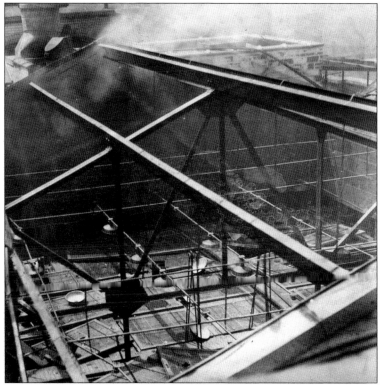

The day might have been worse if the fourth-floor skylight had not blown out; with it gone, ventilation was able to happen as well as the rescue of victims by Cleveland firefighters. The Cleveland Fire Department made gas masks standard equipment for its firefighters after, and because of, the clinic fire. (Courtesy of Special Collections, Michael Schwartz Library, Cleveland State University.)

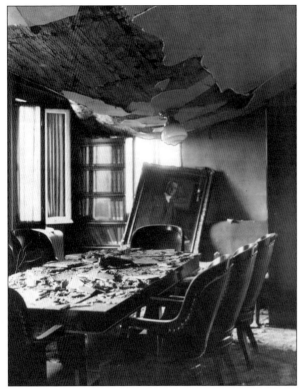

The clinic building was severely damaged, and no effort was made to save it in the aftermath of the fire and explosion. Within two days of the fire, newspapers were reporting, even trumpeting, that the clinic would be rebuilt. The main building was rebuilt but with a significantly different design. Today, the Cleveland Clinic is among the finest hospitals in the world, having branches in locations as far-flung as Toronto, Las Vegas, and Abu Dhabi. The clinic currently has a staff of 2,800 physicians and scientists and is visited by 4.6 million patients a year. (Both, courtesy of Special Collections, Michael Schwartz Library, Cleveland State University.)

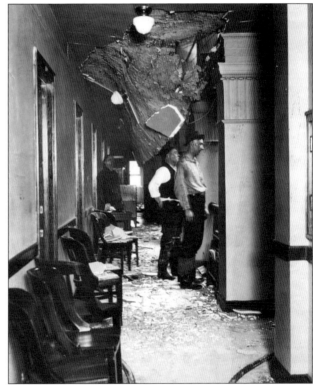

Six
SMOKE ON THE WATER

To label the fires that occurred along the twists and bends comprising the crooked Cuyahoga River as disasters in of themselves is, in retrospect, a bit misguided. Each of the 13 observed fires that sprung forth from their watery nursery are but one facet of a much larger disaster—the immeasurable destruction of the river's ecosystem and subsequent waters of Lake Erie near the mouth of the Cuyahoga River. These blazes, however, represent the most visible and recognizable component of this larger issue. Flames spouting from the waters of a slow-moving river are sensational and headline grabbing, while pictures of industrial sludge oozing from culverts and storm drains are a tad more commonplace. How many metropolitan areas across the nation, let alone the world, can boast a burning river?

Media outlets across the country came to know "the mistake by the lake" and its now infamous river of fire, but few realize that the most notable fire, the blaze of 1969, represents but the last of the aforementioned 13 fires. The burning river earned its nickname from the infernos raging on its waters dating from as far back as 1868.

What happened in Cleveland could have theoretically transpired in any city. Pioneers moved to distant locales, usually establishing a populated area along the nation's rivers and waterways. Before highways, the internal combustion engine, and the steam locomotive, these watery thoroughfares were heavily relied upon to move goods and people from place to place. Logic follows that populous cities and villages along these arteries will succumb to the burdens placed upon it.

In recent years, the Cuyahoga River and its environs have been the focus of a great deal of energy with regards to rejuvenation, reclamation, and redevelopment. Clearly the entire Cuyahoga River valley has weathered the worst of the storm and is in the midst of a major upswing. In this volume the focus is on the fires that further facilitated the river's notorious reputation from 1922 through 1952. Little photographic evidence of the earliest fires exists, while too much has been written about the 1969 blaze.

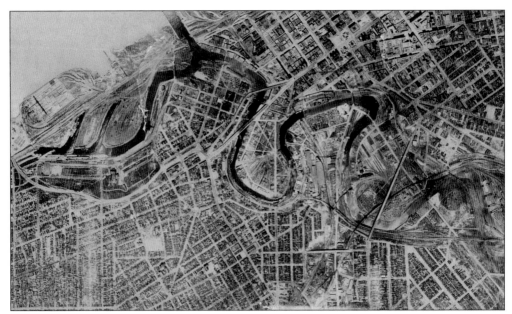

An early aerial view of the crooked Cuyahoga illustrates the industrial presence firmly in place along the river's every bend. While this photograph dates to 1925, fires on the river have been a reoccurring theme since the 1800s. The waters of a flowing river slow along the inside curve of each bend, permitting the accumulation and subsequent ignition of oil and flammable debris to occur. (Courtesy of Special Collections, Michael Schwartz Library, Cleveland State University.)

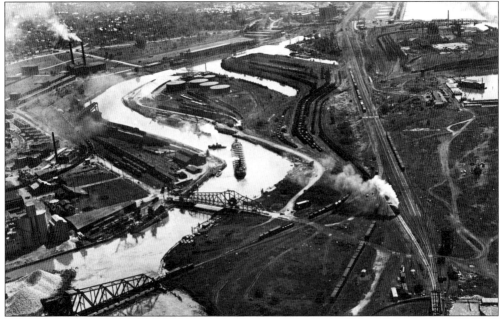

Ships navigated the tight turns of the Cuyahoga River with the aid of a tug while heavy manufacturing belched smoke and particulate into the atmosphere. Standard Oil, pictured here, once relied upon this heavily trafficked waterway to transport the very substance that directly led to many of the river fires that became so synonymous with Cleveland. (Courtesy of Special Collections, Michael Schwartz Library, Cleveland State University.)

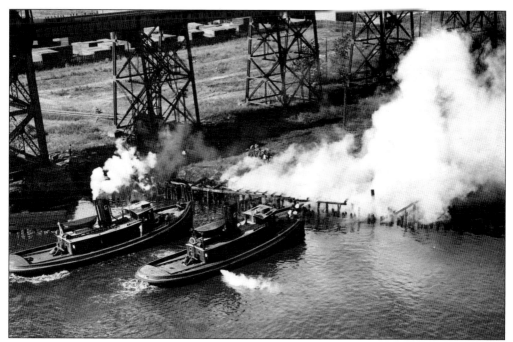

In September 1933, a fire broke out at the old wharf on the Cuyahoga River under the Central Viaduct, due undoubtedly to the steady stream of pollutants so casually deposited daily into the murky waters. The crews of a couple of tugs that fortunately were passing by when the blaze ignited extinguished the fire. Cleveland firefighters arrived just moments after the fire was doused. (Courtesy of the Cleveland Public Library Photograph Collection.)

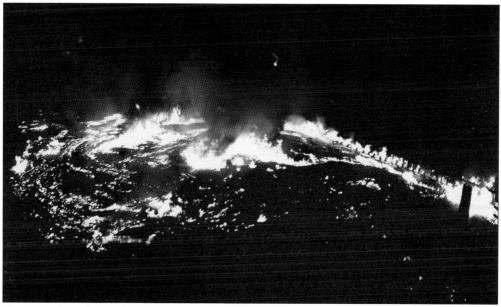

Flames and smoke reach into the nocturnal abyss as the fuel for the blaze swirls in tandem with the currents of the murky waters below. Amidst the blaze, the presence of a doomed wharf can be observed jutting from the right side of the image. (Courtesy of Special Collections, Michael Schwartz Library, Cleveland State University.)

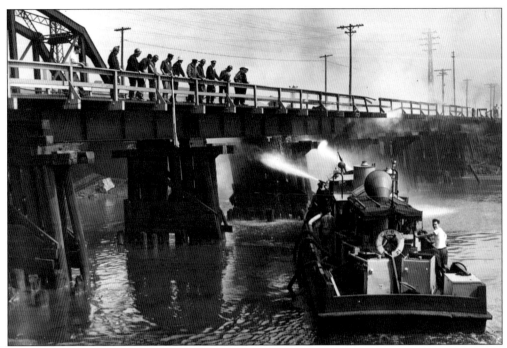

A small company of firefighters observes the last dying gasps of a river fire as it is extinguished by a fireboat in this photograph dated 1949. Damage can be seen to the railing above the tug's smokestack. (Courtesy of Special Collections, Michael Schwartz Library, Cleveland State University.)

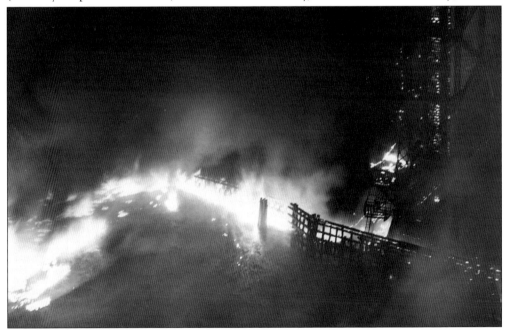

The blaze, which was once dependent upon the chemicals and contaminants within the water to keep it fed, found a new source of nourishment when it made the leap from buoyant debris to permanent structures. The dock and drawbridge are seen here. (Courtesy of Special Collections, Michael Schwartz Library, Cleveland State University.)

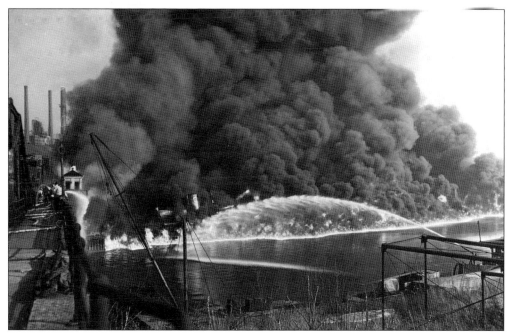

Firefighters as well as a fireboat do the best they can to retard the approaching front of flames while maintaining a relatively safe distance. (Courtesy of Special Collections, Michael Schwartz Library, Cleveland State University.)

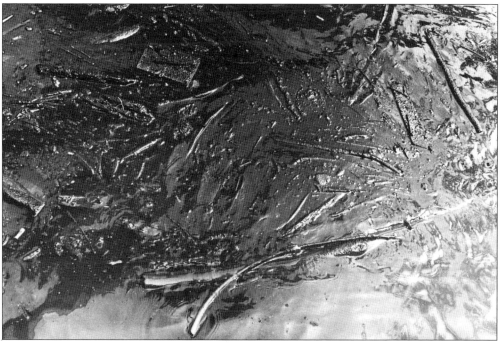

An unnatural sheen coats the surface of these waters, illustrating the totality of man's impact on the aquatic ecosystem in Cleveland's main waterway. The sheer quantity of pollution present in this photograph of the Cuyahoga looks very similar to a tanker spill. (Courtesy of the Western Reserve Fire Museum of Cleveland.)

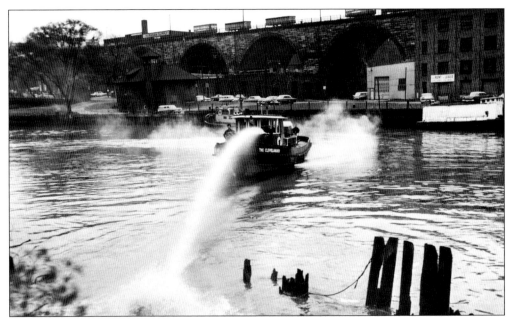

A stout but well-equipped fireboat undertook precautions by eliminating a potentially combustible oil slick along the banks of the Cuyahoga River. While this instance was addressed prior to ignition, such preemptive measures were stretched thin, and other slicks would ignite, whether it be a spark from a passing train or other means. (Courtesy of Special Collections, Michael Schwartz Library, Cleveland State University.)

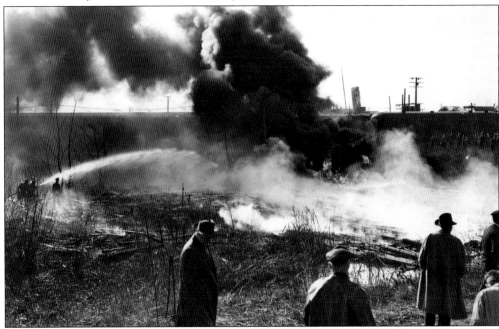

Plumes of noxious black smoke are billowing from a smoldering oil slick. Reporters secured their positions upwind from the scene so that they might commit the events to memory for use later. Firefighters are seen struggling to bring much-needed water to suppress the fire. (Courtesy of Special Collections, Michael Schwartz Library, Cleveland State University.)

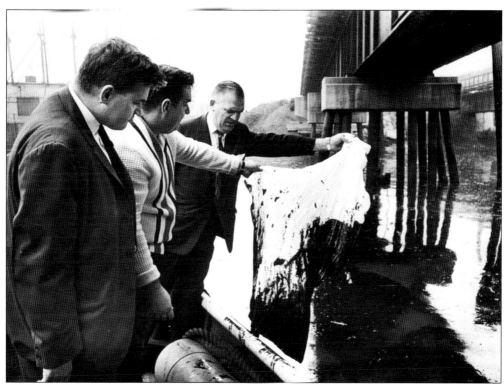

Five years prior to the now infamous burning of the river, city councilmen Sinkiewicz and Katalinas (center) and an unidentified man conducted an informal experiment illustrating the sheer magnitude of oil and pollutants present within the murky waters of the Cuyahoga River. What was once white was easily contaminated with the filth pumped into the city's waterways by adjacent factories, unscrupulous individuals, and surface runoff. (Courtesy of Special Collections, Michael Schwartz Library, Cleveland State University.)

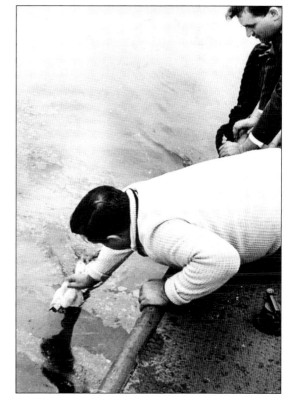

Carefully bracing himself so as not to take an unwanted dip, councilman Edward Katalinas leans over the edge to dip a scrap of white fabric into the oil-laden waters of the Cuyahoga River. (Courtesy of Special Collections, Michael Schwartz Library, Cleveland State University.)

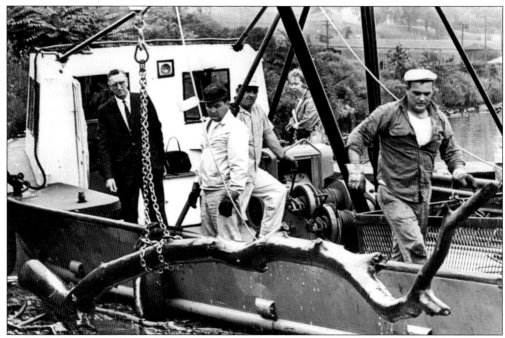

Cleveland mayor Ralph Locher (left) received an up-close view of some of the artery-clogging debris that amassed along many of the bends in the Cuyahoga River. Here, a determined crew and a boat fitted with a winch remove an oil-soaked tree limb from the river's waters. (Courtesy of Special Collections, Michael Schwartz Library, Cleveland State University.)

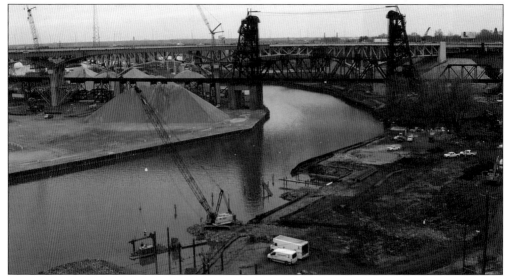

Riverfront lots, once less than coveted and heavily contaminated, now spring to life with new purpose and urgency. The outstretched arms of ever-present cranes carry out the redevelopment. A new stage in the life of the Cuyahoga River is now emerging, and new structures and green spaces will soon come to fruition. What was once an essential artery for the city's economic growth as well as an ongoing source of disgrace is now undergoing an expansive transformation. Bike paths and walkways will soon grace each contour of the crooked river. (Photograph by Kieth Alan Peppers.)

Seven
Death Race 1949

The year 1929 marked the first time the National Air Races were staged in Cleveland with Cleveland Hopkins International Airport serving as the host. Hundreds of thousands of onlookers were thrilled with the sight of these aerial daredevils competing against one another during the early days of aviation. This annual event was electrifying, effectively promoted, and profitable but poorly conceived, as speeding planes whizzed over the ever-increasing suburban sprawl. In retrospect, it seems clear that the National Air Races were destined to lead to death and destruction. Throughout the event's 20-year history, excluding 1939 through 1945 when it was on hiatus due to the war, there were numerous crashes and semi-catastrophes. The tragedy that transpired on September 5, 1949, however, was too horrific to allow the increasingly reckless nature of the spectacle to continue its run in Cleveland.

On a fateful September afternoon in 1949, Bill Odom's F-51 Mustang fighter spun out of control and torpedoed the previously tranquil and safe suburban domicile of the Laird family, killing Jeanne Laird and her 13 month-old-son Craig. Odom, a veteran of World War II, having flown thousands of hours for the Royal Canadian Air Force, was something of a novice when it came to air racing. To make matters worse, Odom had only the slightest amount of experience piloting the plane he flew that fateful afternoon. Jacqueline Cochran, the famed female aviator who was the first woman to fly a bomber across the Atlantic, loaned her plane, the *Beguine*, to Odom for the Thompson Trophy Race. The *Beguine* was not designed for the seven-pylon race that Odom was entered in, and all of these mitigating factors led to the deaths of Odom and a mother and her son.

The National Air Races vacated the Cleveland skyline after that tragic afternoon in 1949, but ever since the late 1960s, the Cleveland National Air Show has continued to bring the finest in aviation to Northeast Ohio, including the first baton pass between wing walkers and the first Ohio appearance of the British Airways Concorde. The air show has become an annual Cleveland Labor Day weekend tradition, attracting over 100,000 spectators and aviators from all over the world, and the unmistakable roar of jets and the flashing glimpse of wings can be witnessed over Cleveland-area neighborhoods by residents.

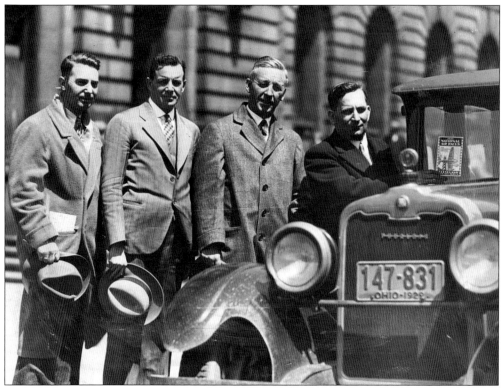

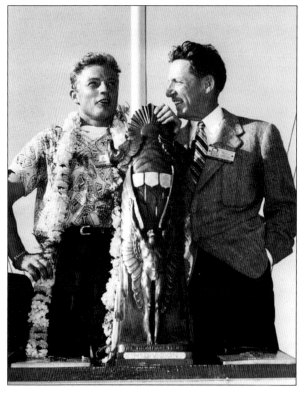

The first man to champion and publicize the National Air Races in Cleveland was the Honorable Mayor John Marshall. Pictured are, from left to right, John Marshall, Clifford Henderson (manager of the National Air Races), Floyd J. Logan (president of the Cleveland chapter of the National Aeronautical Association and chairman of the races), and Alva Bradley (president of the Cleveland Air Races and Aeronautical Exposition Corporation). (Courtesy of Special Collections, Michael Schwartz Library, Cleveland State University.)

Thompson Products Co. was the major sponsor of the Thompson Trophy Races. Standing on the right, Frederick E. Crawford, president of Thompson Products, congratulates one of the last victors of the race, Anson Johnson, in 1948. (Courtesy of Special Collections, Michael Schwartz Library, Cleveland State University.)

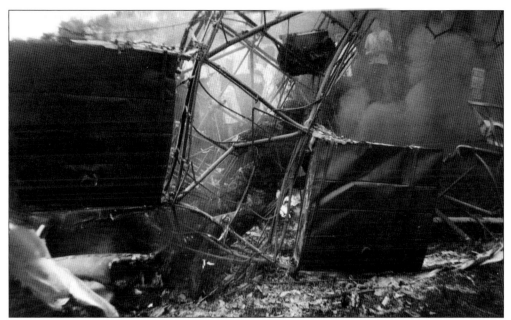

An unidentified aircraft was rendered a heap of scrap metal upon impact. Accidents were a mere formality in the 20-year history of the Cleveland Air Races, peaking in 1947, when nine crashes occurred. The most severe crash during the 1947 campaign involved four airplanes and the death of one pilot, Tony Jannazo, whose aircraft smashed into an open field in Strongsville. (Courtesy of Special Collections, Michael Schwartz Library, Cleveland State University.)

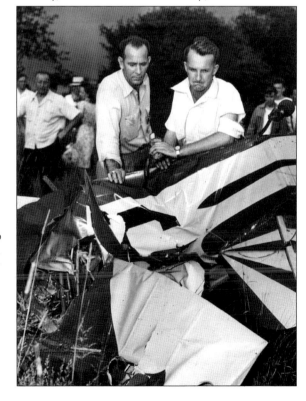

Pilot Claude P. Smith was fortunate to be alive and unscathed after the crash of his aircraft during the National Air Races. He had to bail out when his plane suffered an in-flight structural failure. In this photograph, Smith (right) and Robert J. Hopkins (left), the owner of the plane, survey the damage. (Courtesy of Special Collections, Michael Schwartz Library, Cleveland State University.)

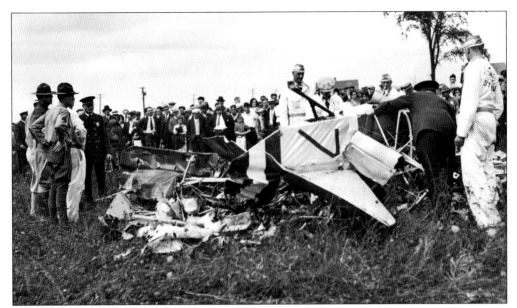

Police officers and air race officials inspect the unidentified debris crumpled among the weeds and tall grasses. Whether it was the flying prowess of the pilot or divine intervention, the pilot and his hurdling missile managed to avoid compounding the matter by avoiding a collision with people and homes. (Courtesy of Special Collections, Michael Schwartz Library, Cleveland State University.)

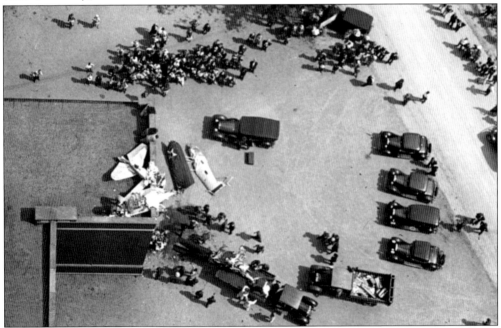

A marine plane crashed atop a school roof after a midair collision with another marine plane during the air races on August 30, 1931. Miraculously the pilots of both wrecked planes, Lts. Lawson H. Sanderson and W. O. Brice, safely parachuted prior to their making deadly impact with roof. They were performing tactical maneuvers at the moment of the mishap. (Courtesy of Special Collections, Michael Schwartz Library, Cleveland State University.)

Here is a map of the 1949 racecourse for the final National Air Races held in Cleveland. The course traversed the skies over budding suburbs such as Middleburg Heights and Berea, the site of the fateful crash that signaled the death knell for the races in Cleveland. (Courtesy of Special Collections, Michael Schwartz Library, Cleveland State University.)

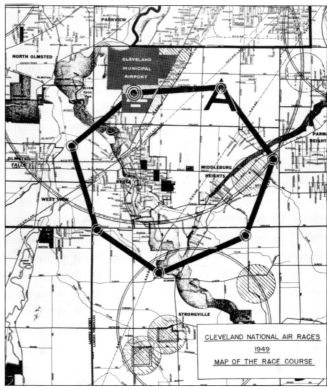

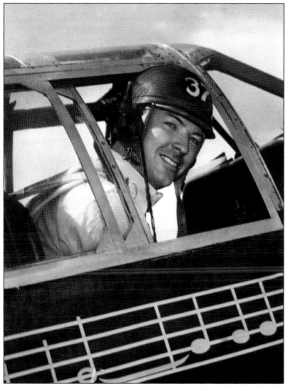

Bill Odom, pictured here in the cockpit of his plane around 1949, was a record-setting flier and one of the most famous aviators in the world at the time of his death. In 1947, he piloted a record-breaking flight, covering 20,020 miles in 78 hours and 55 minutes. (Courtesy of Special Collections, Michael Schwartz Library, Cleveland State University.)

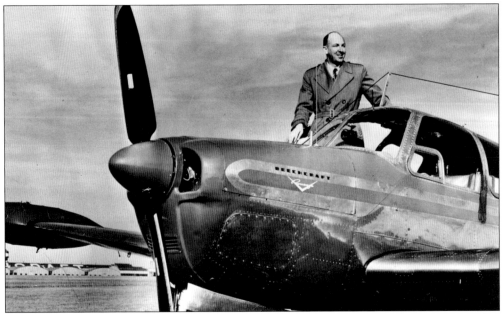

Bill Odom is about to take off for a trial run in his standard Beechcraft Bonanza on December 29, 1948. In a month's time, he and the Bonanza would break the world record for light plane long-distance flying. The Bonanza has an extremely unusual feature: a system of bungee cords interconnecting the yoke and rudder pedals to help keep the plane in synchronized flight during turns. (Courtesy of Special Collections, Michael Schwartz Library, Cleveland State University.)

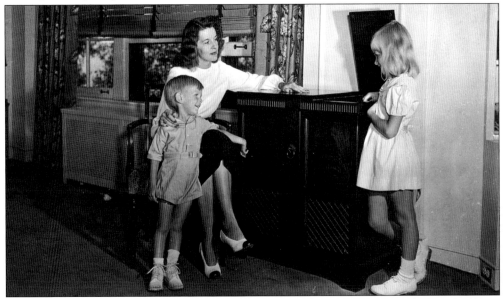

Odom's family attentively listens to a radio broadcast of the prestigious Bendix Trophy Race, pitting ace flyers in a fiercely contested transcontinental competition from Los Angeles to Cleveland. Odom would reign supreme in the 1949 edition. Hopefully, his wife, Nancy, and children, Ronald (age three) and Rochelle (age six) did not tune in for his subsequent contest, the ill-fated Thompson Trophy Race. (Courtesy of Special Collections, Michael Schwartz Library, Cleveland State University.)

Udom shook hands with Jacqueline Cochran, his beneficiary and a world-renowned aviatrix, following his victory in the Sohio Trophy Race on the first day of the National Air Races, September 3, 1949. He flew Cochran's plane in the race and would do so once more in his final competition in four days' time. (Courtesy of Special Collections, Michael Schwartz Library, Cleveland State University.)

Jacqueline Cochran founded and directed the Women's Air Force Service program during World War II. Among her ample achievements, she was the first female to fly faster than the speed of sound and was awarded the Distinguished Flying Medal by the US Air Force in 1969. On March 9, 1996, the US Postal Service issued a 50¢ stamp commemorating her life and achievements. Cochran is depicted on the stamp after winning the 1938 Bendix Trophy air race from Los Angeles to Cleveland in a mere eight hours. (From the archives of the International Women's Air and Space Museum, Cleveland.)

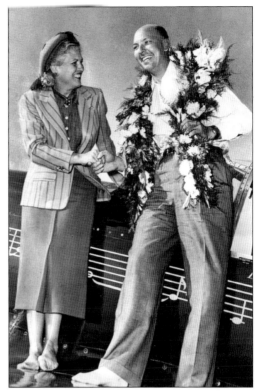

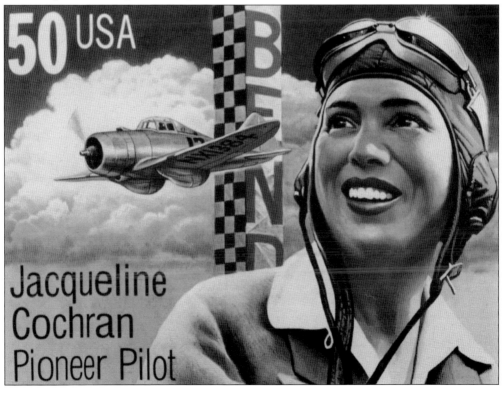

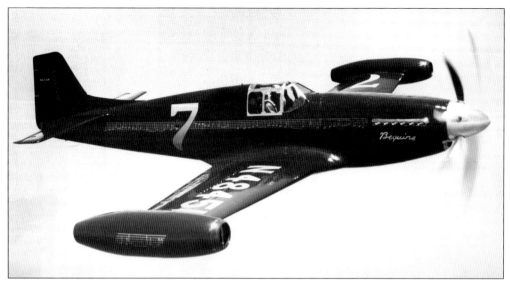

Odom is pictured piloting *Beguine*, an aircraft he had little experience flying prior to the tragic Thompson Trophy Race. In fact, Odom had almost no experience flying in a pylon race such as the Thompson Trophy competition. *Beguine* was a state-of-the-art P-51-C Mustang, radically modified with the glycol and oil radiators moved from the belly of the airframe to the wing tips and encased in pods. The intent was to reduce drag and add range for longer courses. (Courtesy of Special Collections, Michael Schwartz Library, Cleveland State University.)

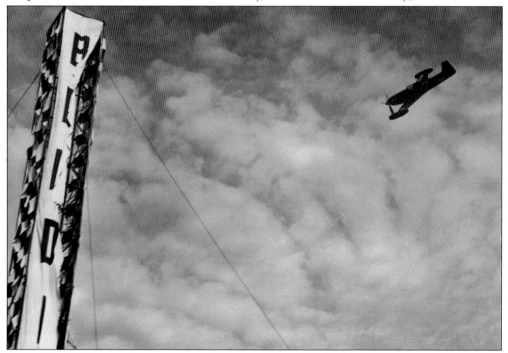

Beguine hurled downward just moments before nose-diving into the Laird's suburban home, taking the lives of Odom, a young mother, and her infant child while a helpless husband could only watch as his family was incinerated and a lifetime of sorrow was sown in the blink of an eye. (Courtesy of Special Collections, Michael Schwartz Library, Cleveland State University.)

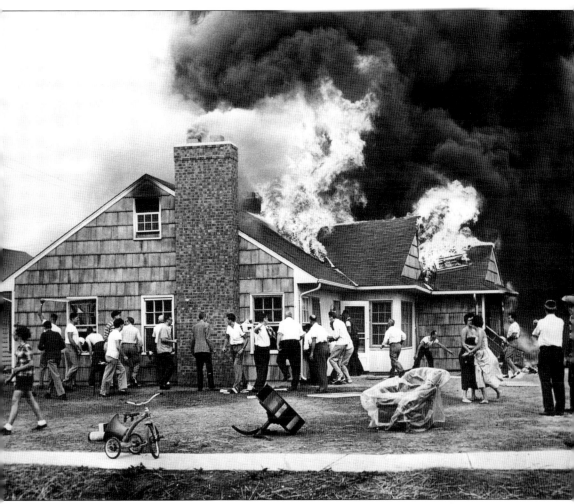

Panic and horror suddenly overwhelmed a previously serene suburban household and neighborhood. Neighbors raced to the aid of the Laird family, but their selfless actions were all for naught as Odom and Jeanne Laird were killed upon impact. Unlike his adoring mother, 13-month-old Craig Laird suffered greatly as his small frame was set ablaze while he sat in his playpen. He was rushed to the hospital where he would succumb to his fatal injuries. This horrifying photograph was taken merely five minutes after impact. (Courtesy of Special Collections, Michael Schwartz Library, Cleveland State University.)

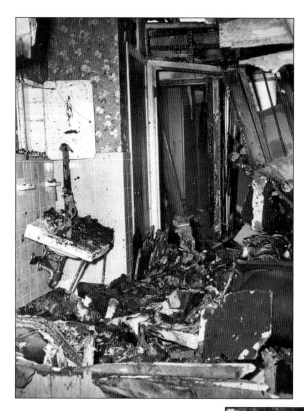

The interior of the Lairds' home offers no glimpse of the sunny, joy-filled familial scenes that played out daily between the young couple and their infant son. Only darkness and destruction now resided in the fractured suburban domicile. (Courtesy of Special Collections, Michael Schwartz Library, Cleveland State University.)

Workers examine the fragments of the wrecked P-51 that Odom failed to maintain control of; a thankless and disheartening task none of these men could have envisioned performing in the hours before the disaster. Nothing could have prepared them for the ashen debris reminiscent of the fallout from a firebombed building in Dresden during World War II. (Courtesy of Special Collections, Michael Schwartz Library, Cleveland State University.)

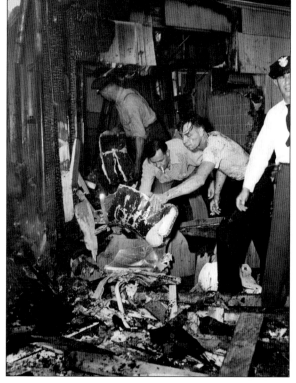

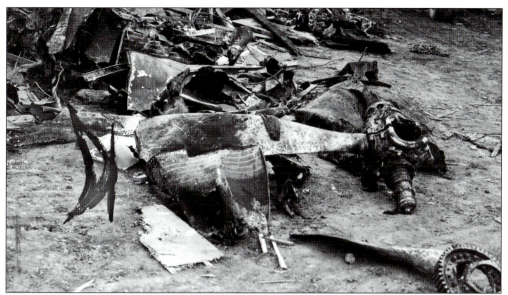

The tattered remnants of the Lairds' defunct American dream lay strewn about. Seared scraps of a formerly blissful suburban setting are scattered among the ashes and scorched earth. (Courtesy of Special Collections, Michael Schwartz Library, Cleveland State University.)

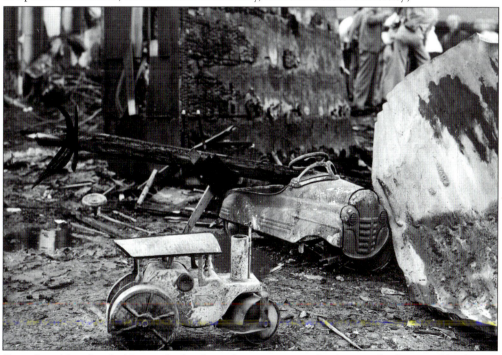

Craig Laird lived only 13 months but brought an eons worth of joy to the hearts of his loving parents. He was at play in his playpen when the crash occurred and ensuing fire torched his tiny frame. His grandfather Benjamin Hoffman grabbed his burning body, frantically tearing off the clothes in attempt to save his life, but alas, the valiant effort failed. Craig's toys are pictured here in the rubble following the horrific plane crash. (Courtesy of Special Collections, Michael Schwartz Library, Cleveland State University.)

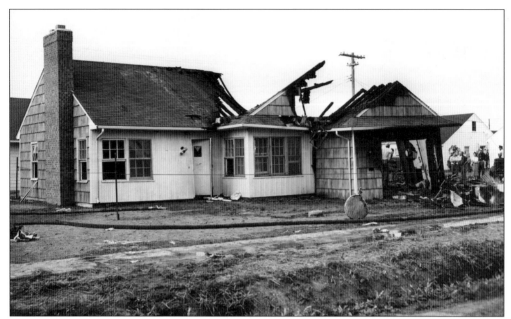

The burned-out residence of the Laird family only slightly articulates the enormity of the horrors that transpired at this site just a few days prior. The 1949 National Air Races were the deadliest in the event's illustrious existence with five deaths in total. The loss felt during that fateful afternoon was the most costly and was the catalyst for ending the races' run in Cleveland. (Courtesy of Special Collections, Michael Schwartz Library, Cleveland State University.)

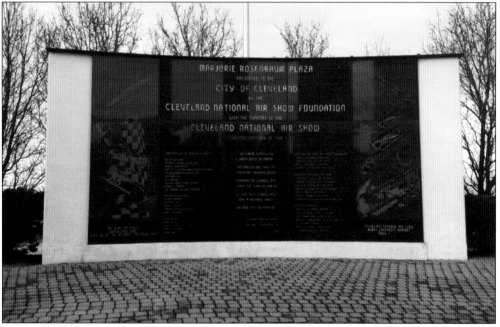

Today, the Cleveland Air Show prospers as it enthralls and delights without placing adoring patrons in peril. Tens of thousands devotees flock to the event every Labor Day weekend to witness the aerial expertise of the Blue Angels, US Navy Leap Frogs, and many more elite pilots and aircraft. (Courtesy of Kieth Alan Peppers.)

Eight

THE DAY THE SHOW DID NOT GO ON

Very few family outings compare to a day at the circus, especially when it is the world-renowned Ringling Bros. and Barnum & Bailey Circus. Unfortunately, in the late summer of 1942, the circus's stop in Cleveland included not just entertainment, but also what should have been a very avoidable tragedy.

The Ringling Bros. and Barnum & Bailey Circus was preparing for the second day of shows, part of a four-day engagement, near the corner of East Ninth Street and Lakeside Avenue when tragedy struck on August 4, 1942.

The fire started a little before noon when reportedly some straw on the west end of the menagerie tent caught fire. Some newspaper reports at the time claimed the fire originated on top of an animal's cage. Regardless of how and why, the fire quickly spread to the paraffin-and-benzene-coated tent (a very common mixture used to waterproof at the time with the added benefit of the perfumed smell of benzene) and was aided by the amount of hay and straw strewn through the tent.

Considering the troupe amounted to over 1,000 animals and 800 performers and staff as well as the flammable surroundings of the circus, the fire could have been much worse. Accounts from the time claim roughly 5,000 spectators gathered to watch the circus employees and Cleveland Fire Department fight the blaze. Quickly put out, by all accounts in under 30 minutes, the fire never reached the big top or any other tents and did not take a single human life due to the efforts of the firefighters and a fair amount of luck. However, many of the circus animals did perish during or as a result of the blaze. At the time, Cleveland Police estimated they had to shoot 26 animals and some accounts claimed over 100 animals perished. Current estimates put it around 65.

The real tragedy of the 1942 fire was that none of the danger signs were recognized; a significantly larger tragedy occurred in Hartford, Connecticut, just two years later.

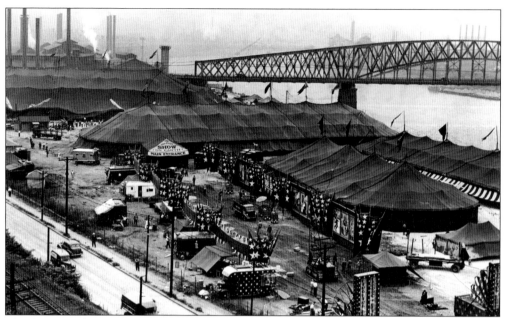

The Greatest Show on Earth would take up a large area when it came to town, as this photograph in Pittsburgh days before the fire illustrates. With its animals and employees outnumbering the population of some villages and towns, tragedies, such as the 1942 fire, would eventually end the big top, moving the troupe to inside arenas. (Courtesy of Special Collections, Michael Schwartz Library, Cleveland State University.)

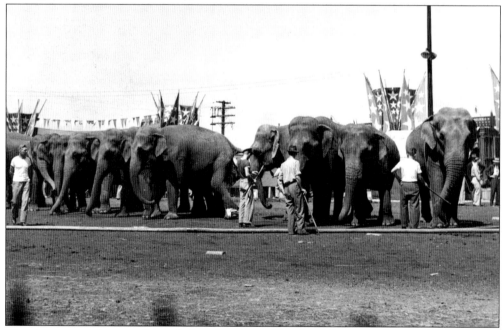

The circus was on its second day of a four-day visit to Cleveland, doing two shows a day at Lakeside Avenue at East Ninth Street. A Ringling Bros. and Barnum & Bailey Circus would come to town with over 1,000 animals and 800 performers. It was one of the biggest events of the summer. (Courtesy of Special Collections, Michael Schwartz Library, Cleveland State University.)

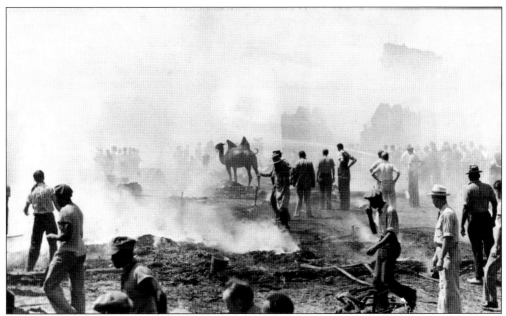

The cause of the fire, originally estimated at $125,000 in damages but ultimately totaling $200,000, was never discovered. In the days after the fire, Pennsylvania police did bring in a suspect who claimed he set the blaze after being fired from the circus. He was ultimately released after too many discrepancies were found in his story. (Courtesy of Special Collections, Michael Schwartz Library, Cleveland State University.)

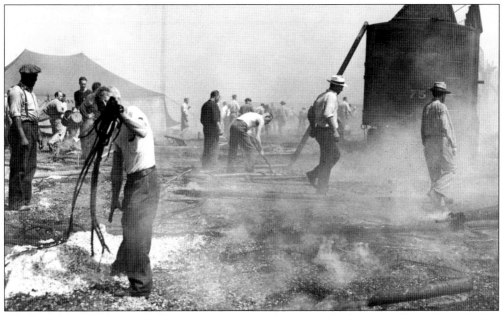

Sideshow venues adjacent to the main tent's entrance were torn down quickly to keep the fire from spreading while some of the other employees of the circus led horses, elephants, and other animals to safety. Still, initial media reports claimed over 100 animals died in the blaze. It is now believed the number killed was 65. (Courtesy of Special Collections, Michael Schwartz Library, Cleveland State University.)

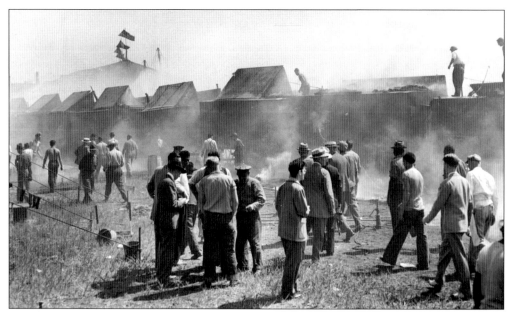

Despite the carnage, there was a performance that evening and during the days following the fire, the carcasses of the animals having been removed from the sight of the patrons. Just hours after the fire, 11,000 people packed the main tent, an increase of 3,000 attendees from the night before, proving the old showbiz adage that the show must go on, especially if the tragedy sells more tickets. (Courtesy of Special Collections, Michael Schwartz Library, Cleveland State University.)

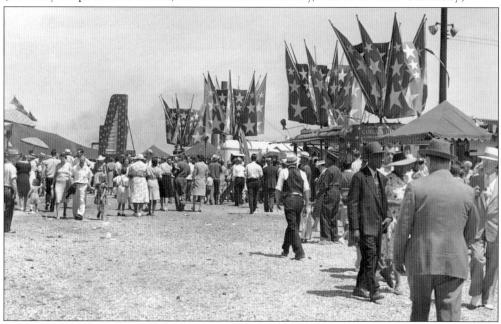

The Ringling Bros. and Barnum & Bailey Circus were big business and always had a large crowd waiting when it pulled into town. In 1942, about four million people attended the show across the nation. Still, wartime conditions forced ownership to employ 25 percent less workers in 1942 than it did in previous years. (Courtesy of Special Collections, Michael Schwartz Library, Cleveland State University.)

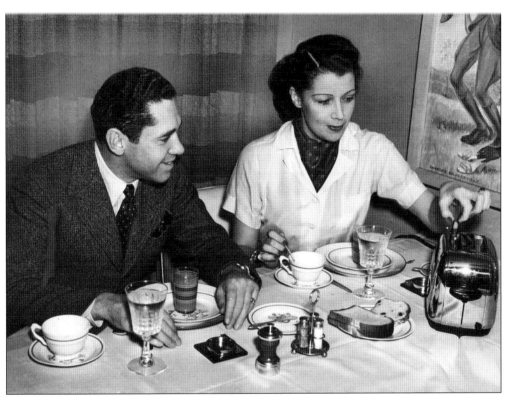

The 1942 fire was not the first time Cleveland had meant trouble for the circus. In 1914, a total of 25 Ringling railroad cars caught fire in Cleveland. Still, although it should not have occurred if wiser heads had prevailed, the fire was unexpected by those present. One of those wiser heads was John Ringling North, pictured. (Courtesy of Special Collections, Michael Schwartz Library, Cleveland State University.)

John Ringling North was the owner of the Ringling Bros. and Barnum & Bailey Circus from 1937 to 1943 and from 1947 to 1967. After the fire, John and his brother Henry, well aware of the lack of safety precautions and manpower, outlined a plan for the board to discontinue performances until the end of the war. He was voted down and resigned. (Courtesy of Special Collections, Michael Schwartz Library, Cleveland State University.)

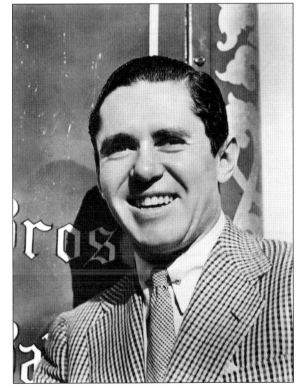

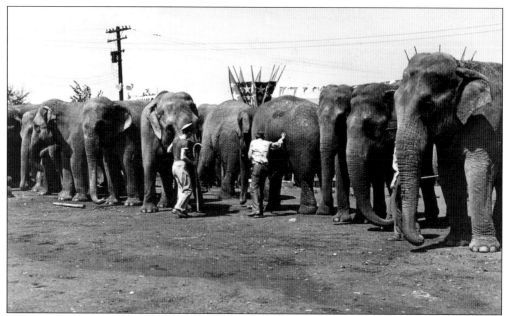

In 1942, fire-resistant technology did exist, but it was new. Like most new technology at that time, the first and often only priority was to use it for the war effort. Because of that, a travelling circus would make do with fire extinguishers under the bleachers and, if possible, brought in pumping trucks, but with the manpower shortage, they were not always fully manned. (Courtesy of Special Collections, Michael Schwartz Library, Cleveland State University.)

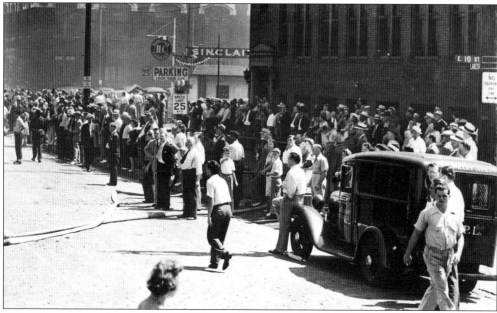

A local newspaper, Lorain County's *Chronicle-Telegram*, reported police cleared Lakeside from East Ninth Street to East Twelfth Street. But by the time the story reached newsprint on the East Coast, police had to handle a crowd of 5,000 who had amassed to see the fire. Regardless of which is true, the short blaze drew a crowd. (Courtesy of Special Collections, Michael Schwartz Library, Cleveland State University.)

According to the *New York Times*, the fire broke out just as the circus employees were sitting down for lunch. But when "Big John" Sabo, the menagerie superintendent, yelled, everyone came running and assisted in putting out the fire. (Courtesy of Special Collections, Michael Schwartz Library, Cleveland State University.)

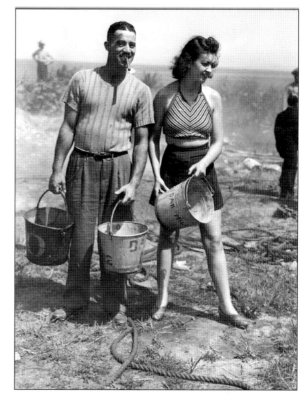

According to several sources, at one point an ostrich with plumes blazing ran from the burning tent. Circus employees who patted out the flames cornered it, and the animal trainers took the bird. One ostrich did perish in the fire. (Courtesy of Special Collections, Michael Schwartz Library, Cleveland State University.)

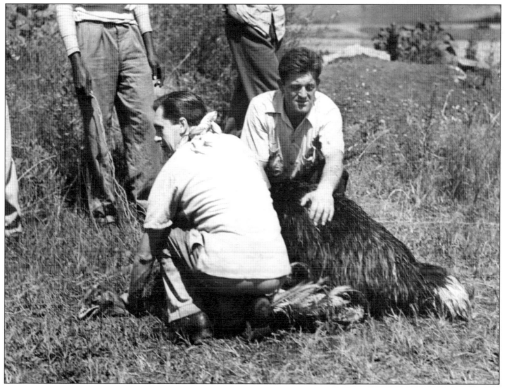

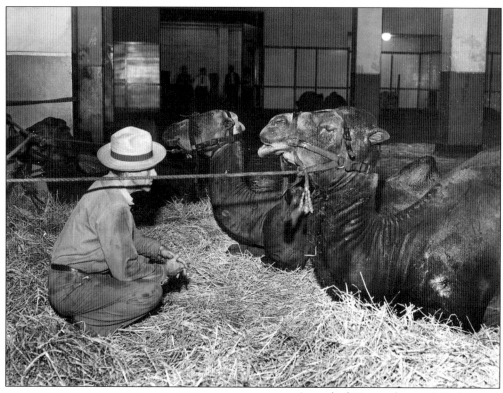

A total of 13 camels were killed in the blaze. Those that survived the initial blaze, along with many of the other animals, were taken to Cleveland's Public Hall for care. Unfortunately three of the camels that survived that blaze still perished. Only two humans suffered injuries. (Courtesy of Special Collections, Michael Schwartz Library, Cleveland State University.)

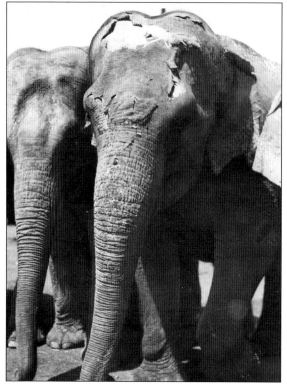

The final count of animals that perished seem to vary from news report to news report at the time, but the final tally probably included 16 monkeys, 13 camels, 12 zebras, 4 lions, 4 elephants, 3 tigers, 3 pumas, 2 giraffes, 2 Indian antelope, an ostrich, and a Indian cow. The carcasses of the dead animals were removed to the Stadler Products Company. (Courtesy of Special Collections, Michael Schwartz Library, Cleveland State University.)

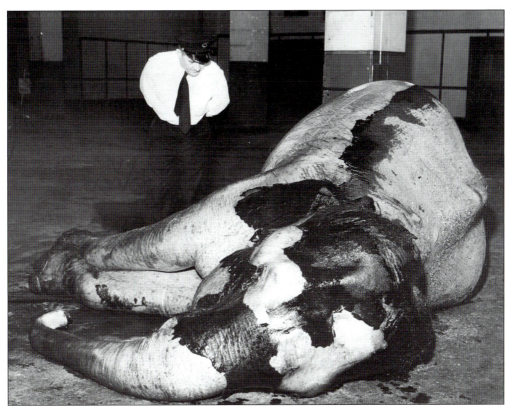

Four of the elephants were blackened to the point of having their ears burned off and their skins simply peeling off their frames. Tragically, they were so well disciplined that they refused to leave the fire until their elephant boss, who suffered burns, led them out of the tent. (Courtesy of Special Collections, Michael Schwartz Library, Cleveland State University.)

As with many occurrences, tall tales grow out of real events. For years, people claimed to remember elephants and giraffes rampaging down East Ninth Street. The truth was less spectacular and more horrific. At the time though, most articles ignored the actual carnage and stressed the survival of Gargantua and Toto, whose wedding ceremony occurred twice daily and who were a national sensation during the summer of 1944. (Courtesy of Special Collections, Michael Schwartz Library, Cleveland State University.)

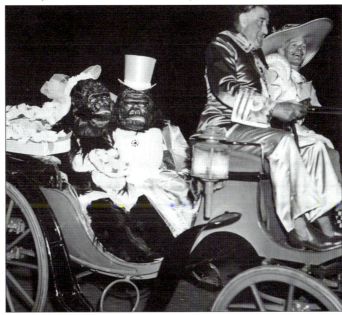

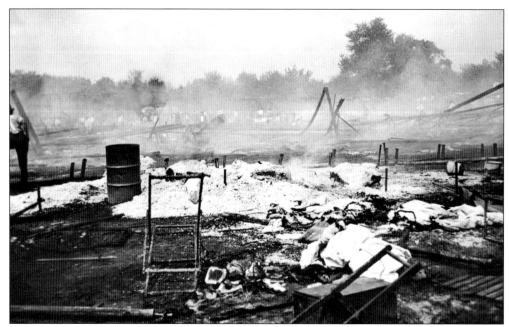

On July 6, 1944, an even larger fire broke out at a Ringling Bros. and Barnum & Bailey Circus in Hartford, Connecticut. It spread quickly in large part because the tents were still being coated in paraffin. Unfortunately, unlike the Cleveland fire, the Hartford fire took place in the big top while 7,000 were attending the Greatest Show on Earth. Somewhere between 165 and 185 perished in the fire; although, some place the tally even higher, and many remain unidentified even today. The outcome of the Hartford fire did force a change in circus safety measures, and members of Ringling Bros. and Barnum & Bailey served time in prison because of negligence. John Ringling North returned in 1947 and headed the circus for another 20 years. (Both, courtesy of Special Collections, Michael Schwartz Library, Cleveland State University.)

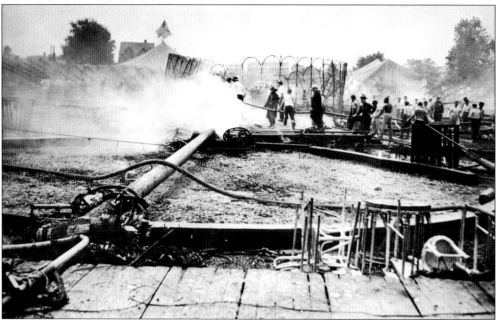

Nine

STREETS OF FIRE

The Cleveland Clinic and Collinwood School fires claimed a higher toll of human life than the events of October 20, 1944. And the Collinwood School fire ended the lives of so many children before they had really even begun them. Even so, the East Ohio Gas Company explosion stands with them as one of the worst disasters in Cleveland history, as it was like a bomb going off and, for a time, laid waste to an entire neighborhood.

The East Ohio Gas Company explosion occurred mid-afternoon at approximately 2:41 p.m. when a tank containing liquid natural gas exploded. Homes, businesses, and the area's residents found themselves engulfed by a tidal wave of fire in which over more than one square mile, or roughly 20 blocks on Cleveland's east side, was laid to waste. The largely ethnic neighborhood, mostly Slovenian, around St. Clair Avenue NE, East Fifty-fifth Street, East Sixty-seventh Street, and the Memorial Shoreway found itself the focus of such carnage that many believed they were under enemy attack.

Before it was over, the neighborhood suffered another large explosion from a second tank as well as a series of much smaller ones and suffered the loss of 79 homes, 2 factories, 217 cars, 7 trailers, and 1 tractor—it also left over 600 residents homeless and claimed 130 lives. Over half of those who perished were unable to be identified since they were burned so badly.

While the fire itself was brought under control somewhere between not long after midnight and midday Saturday, depending on the definition of under control, small fires and minor explosions caused by pockets of gas continued for days.

The residents of the neighborhood began to return Sunday morning and started the grisly search for victims and continued to do so into the middle of November. A mass funeral and burial was held on November 14, with 2,000 people in attendance, in which the 61 unidentified bodies were separately interred at Highland Park Cemetery.

At the epicenter of the disaster now stands Grdina Park, surrounded by a neighborhood rebuilt by residents who would not let their community perish.

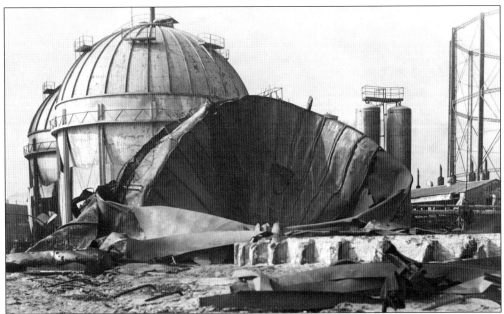

The No. 2 East Ohio Gas Works, a 10-acre facility at St. Clair Avenue and East Fifty-fifth Street, began storing liquefied natural gas in early 1941. It was only the second facility in the county to use a new technology allowing for the storage of 640 more times the volume of natural gas than if it had been left in its original form. (Courtesy of Special Collections, Michael Schwartz Library, Cleveland State University.)

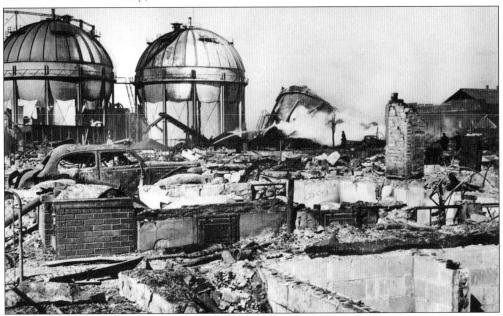

Although a definitive reason for the explosion has never been agreed upon, considering the fourth tank had to be repaired when the inner shell cracked as early as its first use, the different design and use of different materials, as opposed to the three tanks built earlier, were probably a significant part of the subsequent catastrophe. (Courtesy of Special Collections, Michael Schwartz Library, Cleveland State University.)

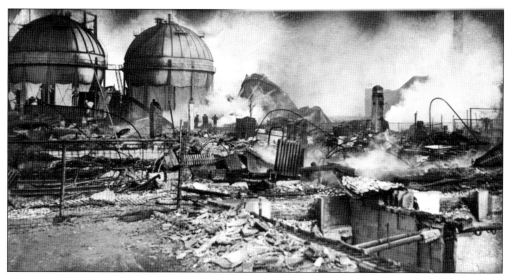

The Nos. 4 and 3 tanks exploded at roughly 2:41 and 3:00 p.m., respectively. A US Bureau of Mines investigation suggested the accident was due to the low temperature of liquid natural gas (-260F) causing the inner tank of No. 4, made with nickel-steel, to become unsound. The nearby railway and plant vibrations probably accelerated the cracking. (Courtesy of Special Collections, Michael Schwartz Library, Cleveland State University.)

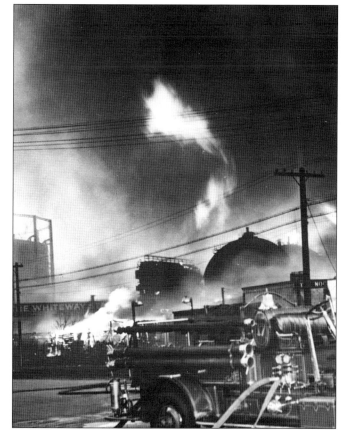

These factors, along with war shortages forcing the use of inferior insulation, led to a leak allowing the liquid natural gas to flow into nearby streets and sewers. Within minutes, the gas met an ignition source and exploded. The ball of flame could be seen at John Adams High School, seven miles away. (Courtesy of Special Collections, Michael Schwartz Library, Cleveland State University.)

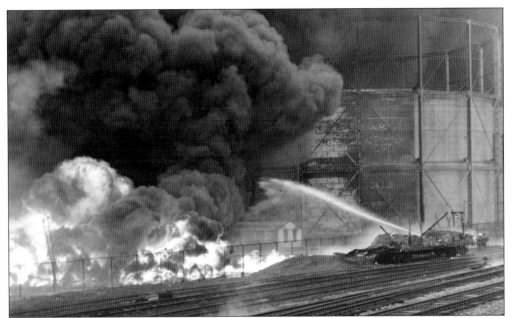

In the moments leading up to the explosion, witnesses reported seeing gaseous clouds, believed to be the gas reverting to its natural state as it escaped storage. A plant engineer later said when he saw white clouds escaping from the tank, he realized the No. 4 tank had let go. Over 70 of his coworkers perished in the blast. (Courtesy of Special Collections, Michael Schwartz Library, Cleveland State University.)

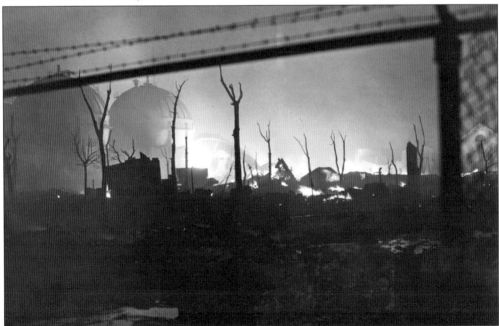

The No. 3 tank exploded about 20 minutes after the first explosion at No. 4 when fires melted the steel supports causing the tank to collapse, ignite, and add to the calamity. Miraculously, the No. 1 and No. 2 tanks did not add to the disaster, staying upright and intact as the fire raged around them. (Courtesy of Special Collections, Michael Schwartz Library, Cleveland State University.)

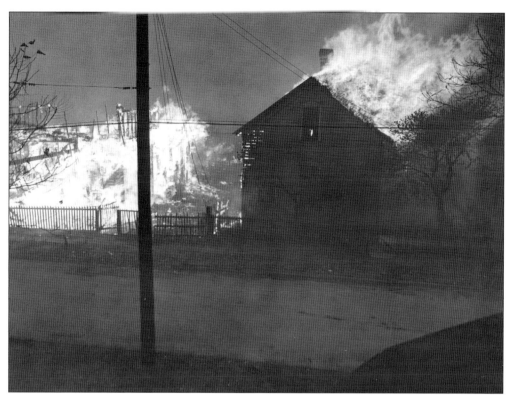

The Cleveland Fire Department responded quickly with the first company arriving on the scene within minutes of the first explosion. They were met by what numerous witnesses described as a war zone. Firefighters were surprised to find even the pavement was on fire. (Courtesy of Special Collections, Michael Schwartz Library, Cleveland State University.)

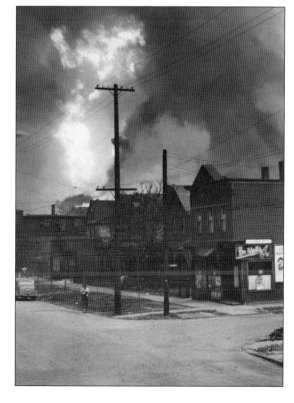

People six miles from the blast site reported feeling the explosion, and the flames were reportedly seen as far away as 25 miles. Newspaper reports at the time reported cars having their tires melted by the intense heat. Office workers across Northeast Ohio have recounted how the heat was so intense that they had to shut their windows in defense. (Courtesy of Special Collections, Michael Schwartz Library, Cleveland State University.)

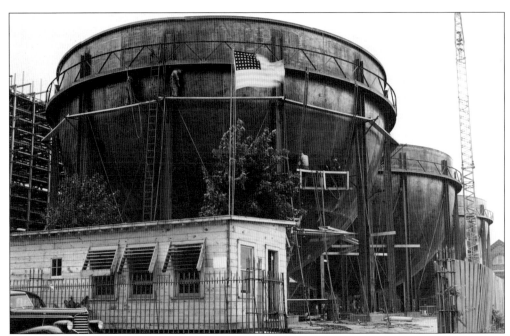

As the natural gas escaped the No. 4 tank, it made its way into the sewer systems of the neighborhood. When the explosion occurred, the natural gas had travelled through and into numerous homes' sewers and basements, turning each dwelling into its own personal inferno. (Courtesy of Special Collections, Michael Schwartz Library, Cleveland State University.)

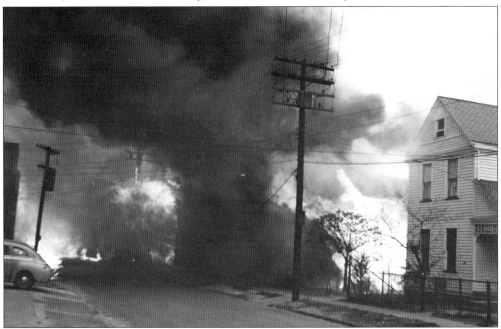

Here is East Sixty-first Street at the height of the fire. The explosion was measured at 130 billion British thermal units. A British thermal unit is a standard form of measurement equal to one wooden match burning. The heat from the blaze was estimated at 3,000 degrees Fahrenheit. (Courtesy of Special Collections, Michael Schwartz Library, Cleveland State University.)

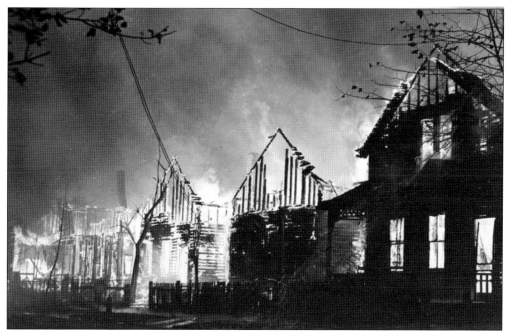

Firefighters also had to deal with the rock wool, which had been used as insulation in the No. 4 tank. The insulation, soaked in the liquid natural gas, was propelled throughout the neighborhood by the blast. (Courtesy of Special Collections, Michael Schwartz Library, Cleveland State University.)

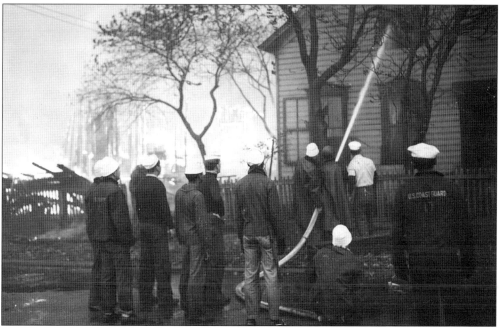

Members of different branches of the US Armed Forces poured into the area to assist. Pictured here, they are fighting the blaze on Lake Avenue using water pumped 1,400 feet via a 1,500-foot hose from Lake Erie by a Coast Guard fireboat. Stopping the fires at this location saved the Ohio Chemical Manufacturing Company from igniting. (Courtesy of Special Collections, Michael Schwartz Library, Cleveland State University.)

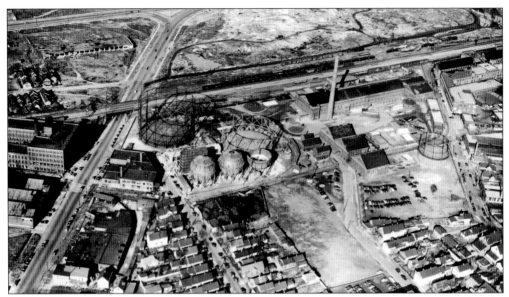

The effect of the blast is evident when comparing an aerial photograph from 1940 to one after the blast while the fires raged. A total of 79 homes were destroyed with another 35 suffering partial destruction. Two plants were destroyed with another 13 suffering significant damage. Added to these totals were 217 automobiles, 7 trailers, and 1 tractor, bringing the cost of the explosion to approximately $8 million in damages. The material losses meant little when compared to 130 lives and another 225 injured, 23 of them being Cleveland firefighters. (Courtesy of Special Collections, Michael Schwartz Library, Cleveland State University.)

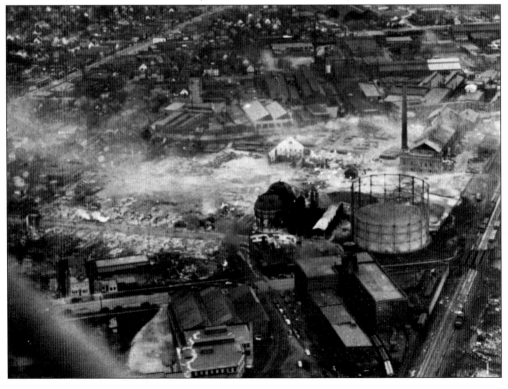

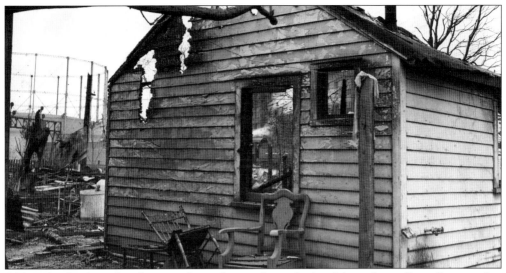

Although it has been decades since the explosion, those who lived through it still vividly remember it. Anne Strazar, then 18, was quoted in a 2004 Cleveland Plain Dealer article on the 60th anniversary of the blast as saying, "I looked at them all the time, wondered what would happen if they exploded. Then, that day, they did. The top blew sky high. There were three or four men on the tank when it exploded. It was horrendous. I thought that the Germans were bombing us, and ran to get away." These photographs, taken 11 days after the explosion, make it fairly evident why she might have thought it was a bombing. (Courtesy of Special Collections, Michael Schwartz Library, Cleveland State University.)

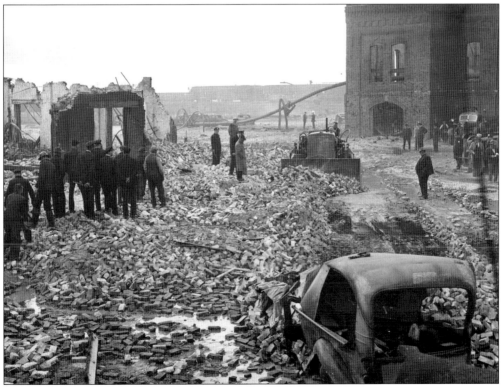

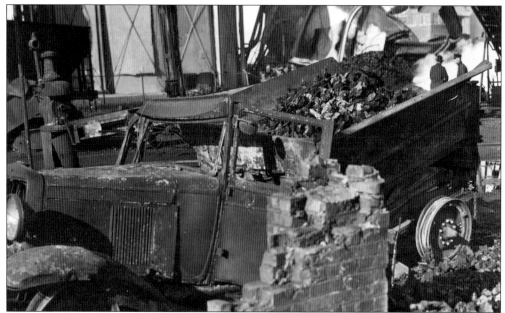

Note that all the tires have been melted off this coal truck from the heat and subsequent fire from the blast. Its owner was among the luckier ones, insurance wise, as according to local lore, some residents had problems filing their insurance claims as the cars they were attempting to file for were melted beyond recognition. (Courtesy of Special Collections, Michael Schwartz Library, Cleveland State University.)

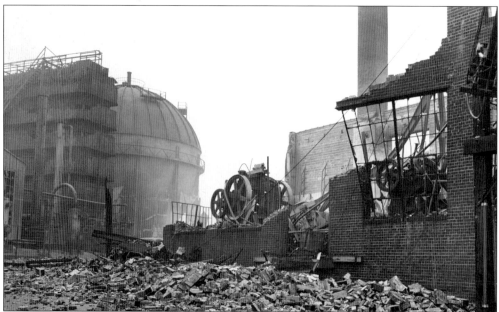

An oddity of the blast was that while some areas around the blast were devastated, others were untouched. These buildings, in the shadow of the plant, almost look as if the walls had been sheared off in a precise manner. Some of the machinery is seemingly intact, while 20 feet away a similar machine was completely destroyed. (Courtesy of Special Collections, Michael Schwartz Library, Cleveland State University.)

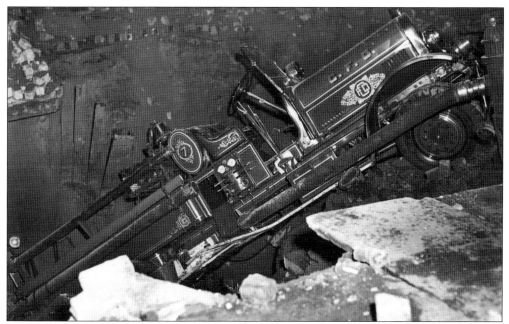
Cleveland Fire Department pumper No. 7 is stuck in a crater at Norwood and St. Clair Avenues. The CFD's response and actions, and those of the city officials in general, were executed with impressive professionalism. With the shortage of water, as the sewer systems had been destroyed, they still managed to bring the fire under control in most of the blast area by midnight. (Courtesy of Special Collections, Michael Schwartz Library, Cleveland State University.)

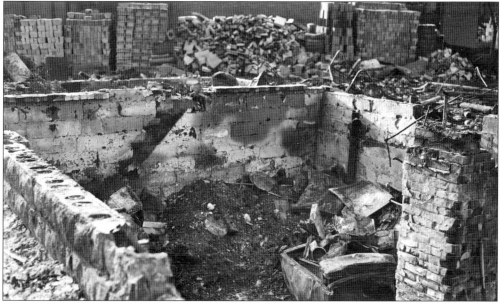
Here is the basement of 1002 East Sixty-first Street where the bodies of Mary Zigman, Josephine Kasic, and Patricia Zigman were found. The amount of lives lost could have been much worse if the blast had occurred 30 minutes later, as the neighborhood's children were in schools just outside the blast range. (Courtesy of Special Collections, Michael Schwartz Library, Cleveland State University.)

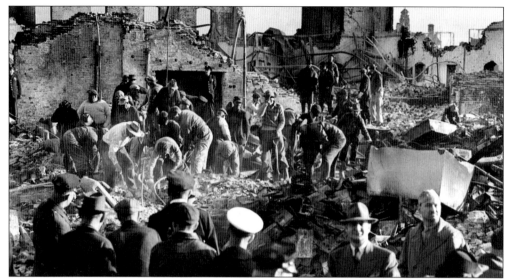

As soon as officials were convinced the area was safe, employees of county engineers office started to search for bodies at the East Ohio Gas Meter Building. Later, as the years went by, there would be claims of numerous bodies found burned beyond recognition in the lockers of the building where they tried to seek refuge from the blast and heat, but there has been little proof that actually occurred. (Courtesy of Special Collections, Michael Schwartz Library, Cleveland State University.)

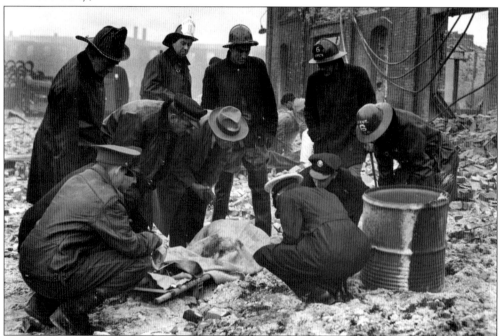

Even if the meter building story was not wholly true, the process of searching for and finding those killed in the disaster was a grisly undertaking. Numerous residents told stories of finding their deceased family members in what remained of their homes. Many victims were found in positions that illustrated their state of panic when the blast occurred. (Courtesy of Special Collections, Michael Schwartz Library, Cleveland State University.)

Employees of the East Ohio Gas Company also conducted themselves admirably in the days after the explosion and fires. Despite having lost 73 of their coworkers to the disaster, gas company employees drained the natural gas from the No. 1 and No. 2 tanks and worked toward stabilizing the area. (Courtesy of Special Collections, Michael Schwartz Library, Cleveland State University.)

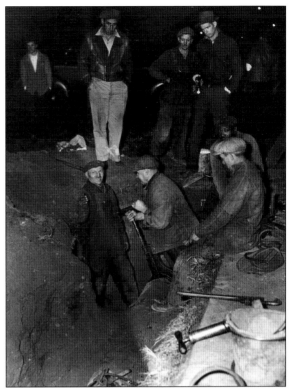

The search for the dead lasted until mid-November. The weather had taken a turn for the worse in early November, and many of the buildings were structurally unsound and dangerous for those inside them. Over 60 of the recovered bodies could not be identified because they were so badly burned or, in some cases, only part of their bodies were found. (Courtesy of Special Collections, Michael Schwartz Library, Cleveland State University.)

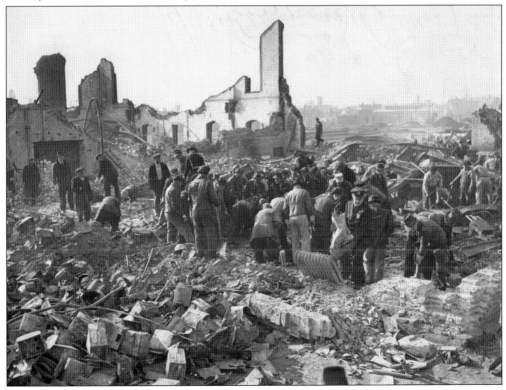

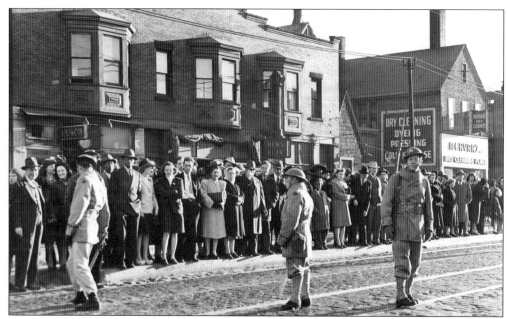

Curious Clevelanders found a way to get glimpses of the area, which was still off limits to nonresidents. In this photograph from October 24, crowds line up to take the trolley at Marquette and East Seventy-ninth Streets. Many supposedly rode the line back and forth as it was the closest view anyone could get to the blast area. (Courtesy of Special Collections, Michael Schwartz Library, Cleveland State University.)

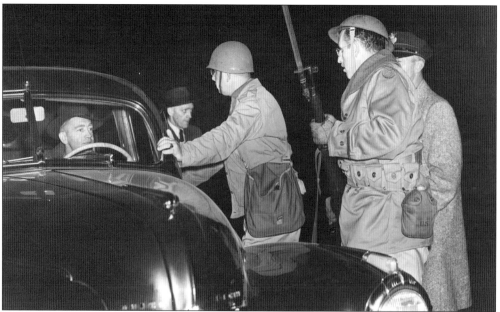

With stories of dead bodies strewn all across the landscape, along with supposedly thousands of birds that had been virtually melted out of the sky, Clevelanders tried to get into the blast area to see the neighborhood themselves. Here, authorities stop a driver trying to enter the area at the East Fifty-fifth Street/Bourne Avenue blockade. (Courtesy of Special Collections, Michael Schwartz Library, Cleveland State University.)

The bank failures of the early 1930s were only a decade in the past, including the failure of one bank in the St. Clair neighborhood. Supposedly, authorities and those searching the area recovered $15,000. The federal government would only replace bills that were at least 3/5 intact. Anything less was up to the discretion the US Treasury Department. (Courtesy of Special Collections, Michael Schwartz Library, Cleveland State University.)

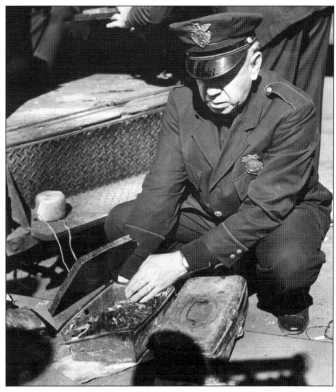

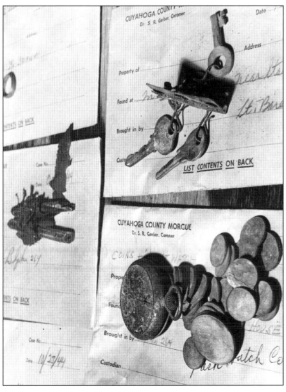

The Cuyahoga County Morgue did as good of a job as possible to make sure valuables were returned to the families of the dead. In some instances, what was worn or carried by the victims was the only way they could be identified. (Courtesy of Special Collections, Michael Schwartz Library, Cleveland State University.)

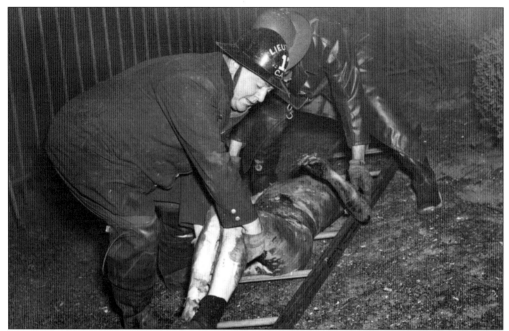

Soldiers, doctors, firemen, and civilians joined in what started out as hopefully a rescue operation but quickly revealed itself as a search for bodies. Carrying bodies from the blockaded area became a fairly regular occurrence in the first few days after the blast. (Courtesy of Special Collections, Michael Schwartz Library, Cleveland State University.)

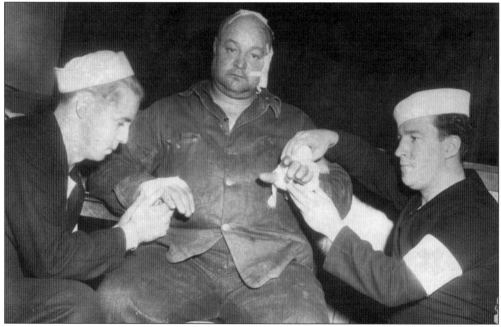

In the hours after the blast, those working in the blast area were able to assist in the medical care of survivors. Here, two sailors are assisting an East Sixty-first Street resident who had literally been blown out of his car by the blast. (Courtesy of Special Collections, Michael Schwartz Library, Cleveland State University.)

The area surrounding the burning blast was evacuated, and the 680 homeless people were sheltered in Willson Junior High School on East Fifty-fifth Street, where the Red Cross tried to care for everyone. In this hallway, a number of children bed down for the night. (Courtesy of Special Collections, Michael Schwartz Library, Cleveland State University.)

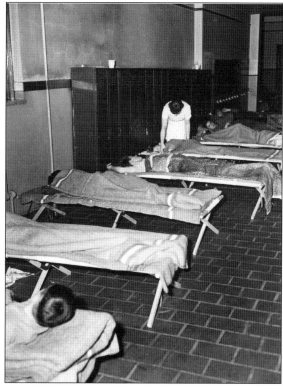

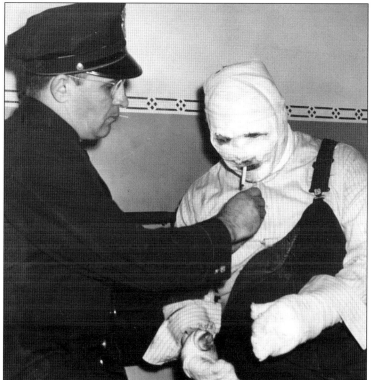

According to the *Cleveland Press*, this photograph shows patrolman Frank Morgan of the 5th District assisting a blast victim who lived on East Sixty-second Street. Many of the surviving victims, like this one, were taken to St. Vincent Charity Hospital, where smoking regulations in hospitals in 1942 were not as strict as they are today. (Courtesy of Special Collections, Michael Schwartz Library, Cleveland State University.)

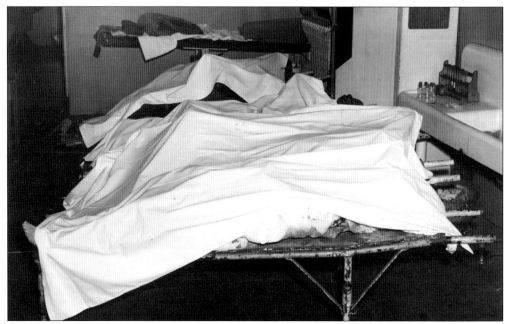

Thankfully, between the hospitals, schools, and the morgue, the latter was the least crowded. However, a disaster that took the life of 130 people still taxed what the Cuyahoga County Morgue was capable of, especially with the daily lines of survivors searching for their family members. (Courtesy of Special Collections, Michael Schwartz Library, Cleveland State University.)

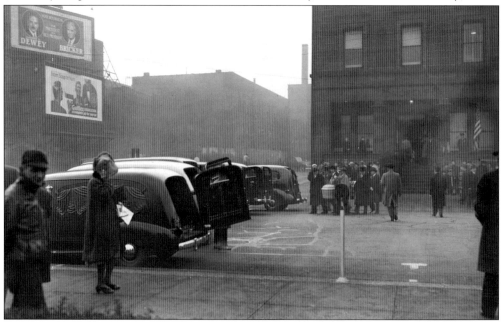

Hearses line up outside the Cuyahoga County Morgue to transport bodies for a mass funeral. Held on November 14, 1944, at Highland Park Cemetery, each of the 61 unidentified bodies received its own casket in an individual burial site. Although often, the unidentified body was only part of a body, as that was all that was recovered. (Courtesy of Special Collections, Michael Schwartz Library, Cleveland State University.)

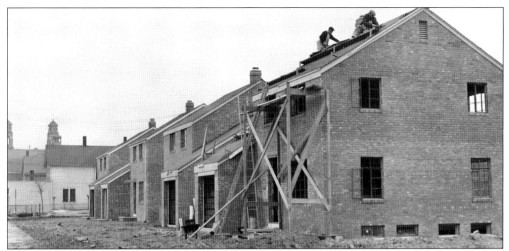

The East Ohio Gas Company paid out over $3.5 million in settlements to the neighborhood around the plant and to its employees. Houses were replaced, and many of the families returned to new homes. The neighborhood did rebound. This photograph shows houses near completion in 1946. (Courtesy of Special Collections, Michael Schwartz Library, Cleveland State University.)

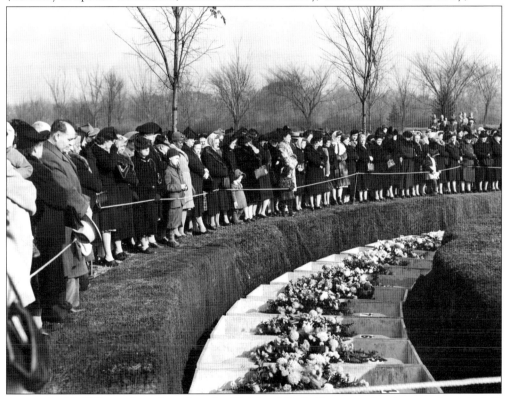

A crowd of 2,000 people gathered at the Highland Park Cemetery for the mass burial of 61 victims—21 of whom were never known by name. Funeral directors donated their services. Every casket and hearse used was also donated. A marker was placed to honor the dead who would never be claimed. (Courtesy of Special Collections, Michael Schwartz Library, Cleveland State University.)

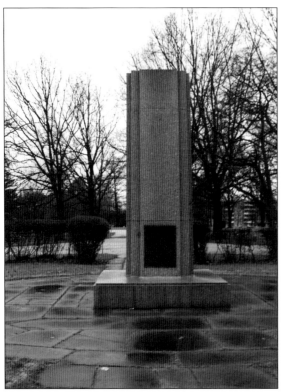

There are two monuments to the victims of the East Ohio Gas Company explosion. At the burial site at Highland Park Cemetery, an obelisk reads, "Social Progress attuned to Industrial achievements for the benefit of the living shall be a memorial to these whose lives were unwittingly sacrificed Oct. 20, 1944." There had been some criticism over the years that the East Ohio Gas Company's part in the tragedy was not mentioned. So in 2007, a second marker at Grdina Park, which stands where the tanks were situated 70 years ago, simply tells the story of what happened that day, including the fact that the East Ohio Gas Company took responsibility for the tragedy and helped rebuild the community. It also tells of how the tragedy changed the way companies stored natural gas across the country. (Both, photograph by Calvin C. Rydbom.)

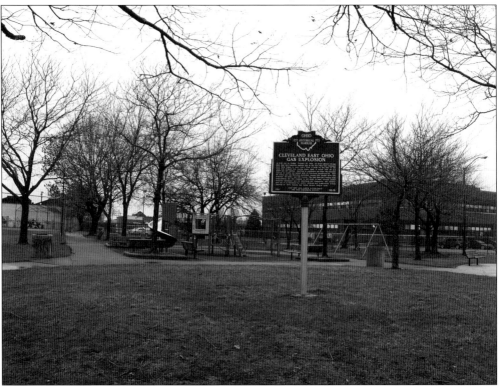

Ten

The Worst Rush Hour in Cleveland History

While thankfully it did not result in nearly the loss of human life as other Cleveland disasters have, when West 117th Street turned itself inside out and upside down in the fall of 1953, the amount of damage and shock caused still earns it a place among Cleveland's most startling and destructive disasters. Then as now, West 117th Street is a well-travelled thoroughfare that crosses both Cleveland and Lakewood and intersects with other major roads such as Madison Avenue, Detroit Road, Berea Road, and Lake Avenue. Many Northeast Ohio residents drive it daily, but curiously, the day the road exploded is more or less forgotten outside the immediate area.

The first explosion, which triggered the events of September 10, 1953, was reported at 5:15 p.m., and within a few seconds, roughly a mile of West 117th Street had been ripped apart with large chunks of the road and manhole covers becoming airborne and returning in not necessarily a place where they had started from. Cars, and the startled people within them, also found themselves flung into their air. Unbelievably, there was only one fatality, although 64 people found themselves in the hospital. A few drivers had to be cut out of their cars by responding police officers and firefighters. Adding up the damage to the street itself and the water, sewer, and gas lines as well as to railroad and trolley lines resulted in a cost of $5 million. The incident also generated 91 personal injury lawsuits totaling another $2.5 million.

Then, as now, it is believed that the explosion occurred due to a number of the 194 different factories dumping their industrial waste and chemicals into the local sewer systems. However, there has never been a definitive answer, even after a special team was set up to study the explosions. But when there is a sewer system full of flammable waste sitting underneath West 117th Street, all that was required was a little spark or even a casually tossed away cigarette or cigar to create this disaster.

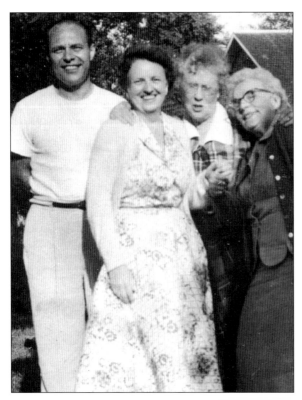

Katherine Szabo, second from the left, was unbelievably the only casualty of the explosion. Her car was hurled into the air by the blast and was crushed by concrete, which fell on her car as it returned to West 117th Street. She and her brother had just driven under the New York Central Overpass when the blast occurred. (Courtesy of Special Collections, Michael Schwartz Library, Cleveland State University.)

The explosion was so fierce it destroyed many of the cars that were unfortunately being driven down West 117th Street as the blast occurred. This car, like many others, found itself surrounded by debris, which had also been blown loose of the street. (Courtesy of Special Collections, Michael Schwartz Library, Cleveland State University.)

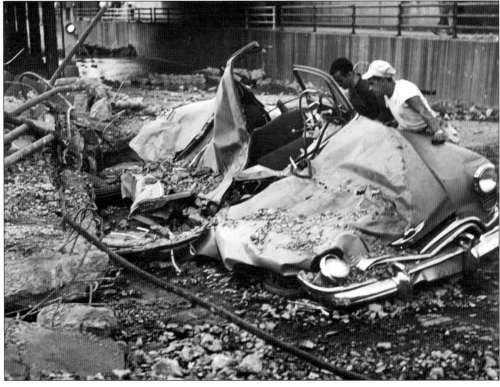

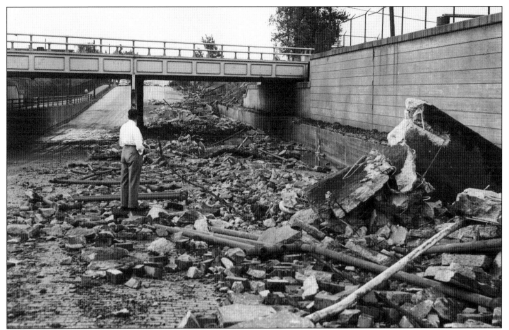

An onlooker surveys the destruction near Madison Avenue. The length of the blast covered 5,000 feet of the road. The bridge in the photograph is the New York Central Overpass and is located near the scene of the explosion's only fatality. (Courtesy of Special Collections, Michael Schwartz Library, Cleveland State University.)

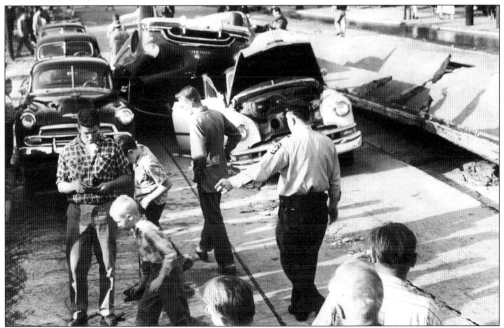

This photograph was taken looking north along West 117th Street between Clifton Boulevard and Lake Avenue. The officer in the photograph, Lakewood's William Leonard, was on patrol duty when the blast occurred. A manhole cover, blown clear off the street, barely missed his cruiser. (Courtesy of Special Collections, Michael Schwartz Library, Cleveland State University.)

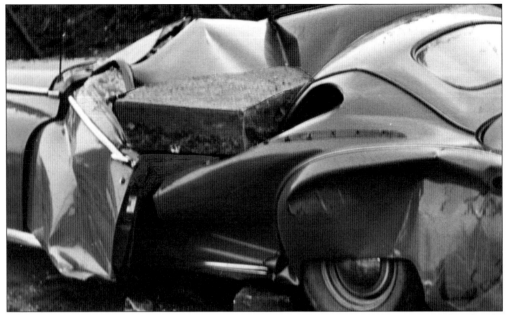

Here, a concrete block crushed a car just south of Madison Avenue. As dangerous as the chunks of concrete were, a considerable amount of damage was done by the 100-pound manhole covers blown off the street. The circular projectiles caused considerable damage to the third and fourth floors of a number of buildings. (Courtesy of Special Collections, Michael Schwartz Library, Cleveland State University.)

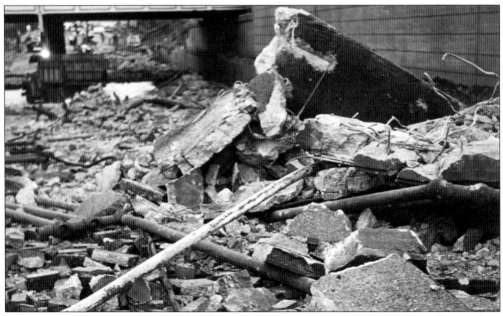

Here is a stretch of road between Madison Avenue and Berea Road. East Ohio Gas workers moved into the area quickly to cap off any gas lines damaged in the explosion. The Red Cross was also busy in the area handing out food and water to those who had little or no access to water or power after the blast. (Courtesy of Special Collections, Michael Schwartz Library, Cleveland State University.)

In only a matter of days, the sewers were being repaired and the streets were being rebuilt. The cost of the damage done was $5 million. Here, workmen with welding equipment and jackhammers labor at repairing rail lines. Both railroad and trolley lines suffered significant damage in the blast. (Courtesy of Special Collections, Michael Schwartz Library, Cleveland State University.)

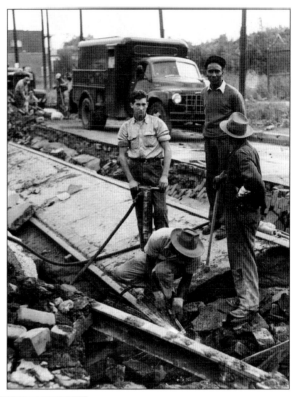

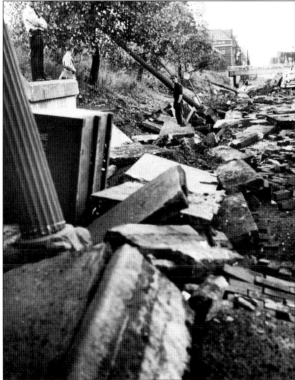

Policeman are surveying the damage not far from Berea Road. A few workers of the White Motor Company, a Cleveland firm specializing in buses and large vehicles, were injured near this spot waiting for a bus. (Courtesy of Special Collections, Michael Schwartz Library, Cleveland State University.)

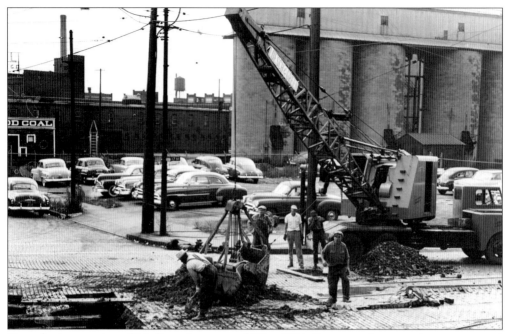

Near the intersection of Madison Avenue and West 117th Street, workers repair a cave created by the blast while in the shadow of a few of the almost 200 businesses that surrounded the blast area. Some of these businesses would eventually be blamed for the explosion. (Courtesy of Special Collections, Michael Schwartz Library, Cleveland State University.)

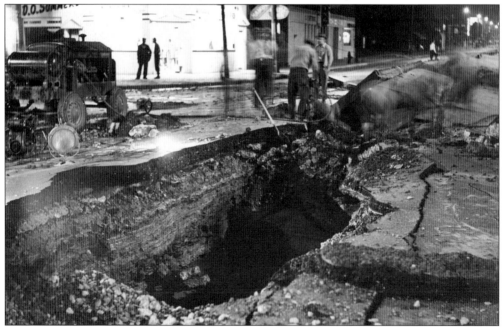

The sewer system under West 117th Street was rebuilt in a week's time, as workers toiled day and night. In the background is one of the then 50-plus locations of D.O. Summers, one of the oldest retailers in Cleveland still operating, having opened its doors in 1881. (Courtesy of Special Collections, Michael Schwartz Library, Cleveland State University.)

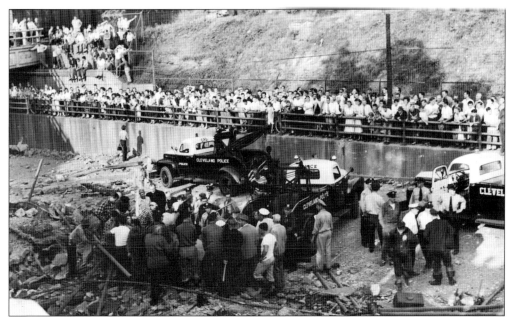

Cleveland mayor Thomas Burke, who later served as a US senator from Ohio and for whom Burke Lakefront Airport is named, urged citizens to avoid the blast area so as not to hinder the rescue work. Not many listened if this photograph between Berea Street and Madison Avenue is any indication. (Courtesy of Special Collections, Michael Schwartz Library, Cleveland State University.)

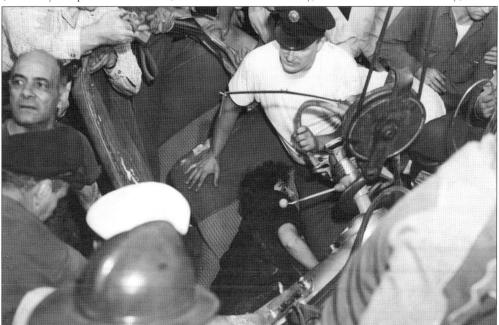

Firefighters, police, and other workers struggle to free Eleanor Rinaldi. She had been trapped by concrete, which had crushed the dashboard of the car and trapped her legs. The situation was so severe that a local priest administered last rites; thankfully, she survived, remembering nothing of the ordeal. (Courtesy of Special Collections, Michael Schwartz Library, Cleveland State University.)

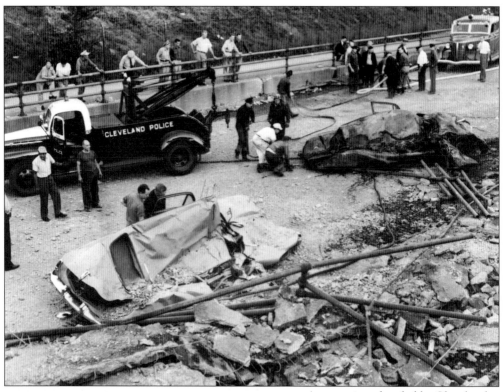

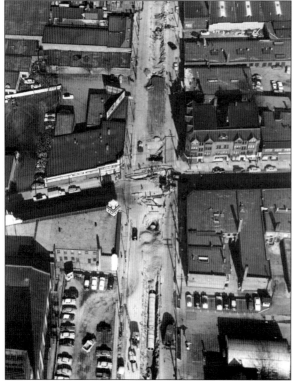

A committee headed by Cleveland coroner Sam Gerber and consisting of Dr. George Barnes, Dr. Leon Weinberger, and Prof. George Blum from the Case Institute of Technology was formed to investigate the cause of the explosion. They also received assistance from departments of the US government during the investigation. (Courtesy of Special Collections, Michael Schwartz Library, Cleveland State University.)

The aptly named *Report on the Investigation of the West 117th Street Sewer Explosion of September 10, 1953*, written by Dr. Barnes and Professor Blum, focused on the many plants seen in this photograph and the belief they had been illegally dumping their chemical and industrial wastes into the sewer system. (Courtesy of Special Collections, Michael Schwartz Library, Cleveland State University.)

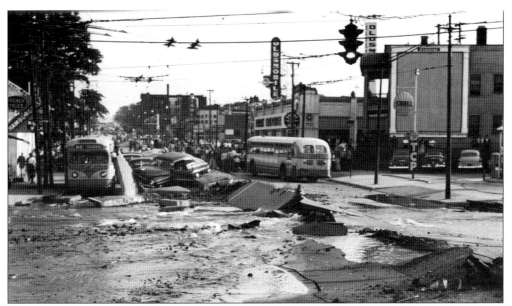

Pictured is the corner of West 117th Street and Lake Avenue. Along with showers of concrete, manhole covers, and debris, the explosion also damaged water lines and caused flooding in parts of the blast area. The Red Cross brought water for the damaged water lines. (Courtesy of Special Collections, Michael Schwartz Library, Cleveland State University.)

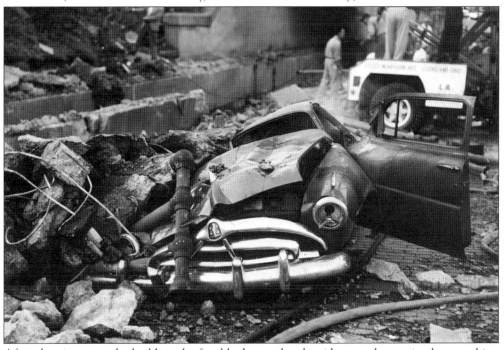

After cleaning up and rebuilding the five-block area, local residents and motorists began asking who was responsible for the explosion. Eventually, they filed 91 personal injury lawsuits, totaling $2.5 million, against Ferbert-Schorndofer, Shell Oil, Sun Oil, Union Carbide, White Sewing Machines, and the Cities of Cleveland and Lakewood. (Courtesy of Special Collections, Michael Schwartz Library, Cleveland State University.)

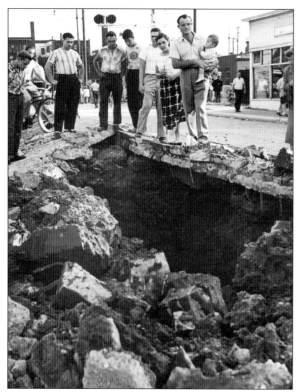

Here is a cave-in just north of the Nickel-Plate Railroad crossing. The plaintiffs and their lawyers accused the companies of dumping illegal waste and flammable substances in the sewers and causing the disaster. They also claimed the Cities of Cleveland and Lakewood were responsible for allowing the conditions that led to the destruction. (Courtesy of Special Collections, Michael Schwartz Library, Cleveland State University.)

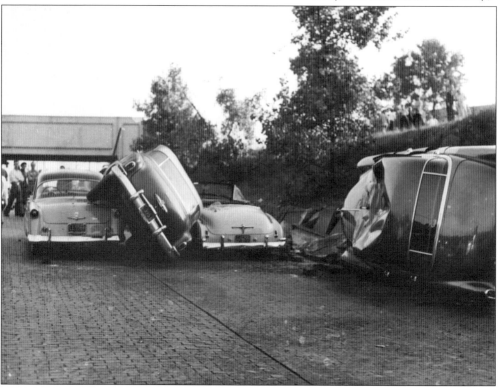

Pictured is an interesting "parking lot" between Berea Street and Madison Avenue. The lawsuits were finally settled via an out-of-court settlement in June 1957. Instead of $2.5 million, the Cities of Cleveland and Lakewood and the five named companies agreed to pay a total of $205,000 and would admit no wrongdoing. (Courtesy of Special Collections, Michael Schwartz Library, Cleveland State University.)

BIBLIOGRAPHY

Bellamy, John Stark. *Cleveland's Greatest Disasters*. Cleveland, OH: Gray & Company, 2009.
Charles, Fred. "Lorain Desolate City, Lift's Eyes to Red Cross Flag as Star of Hope." *Cleveland Plain Dealer*. July 30, 1924.
Cleveland Fire Department. *Cleveland Fire Department 1863–1993*. Cleveland, OH: Taylor Publishing Company, 1995.
Clifford, Robert H. "Tornado Struck Like Giant Claw of Death." *Cleveland Press*. July 28, 1964.
"Crib No. 5 Gives Up Last Four Bodies Of Tunnel's Dead." *Cleveland Plain Dealer*. August 21, 1916.
In Loving Remembrance: Collinwood School Fire Commemorative Booklet. Cleveland, OH: Cleveland Public Library, 2008.
Matowitz Jr., Thomas G. *Cleveland's National Air Races*. Charleston, SC: Arcadia Publishing, 2012.
National Fire Prevention Association. *The Cleveland Clinic Fire*. Boston, MA: NFPA, 1929.
Ramseye, J. Mark. *Ringling Bros.-Barnum & Bailey Combined Shows V. Ringling: Bad Appointments and Empty Core Cycling at the Circus*. Cambridge, MA: Harvard Law School, 2008.
Sangiacomo, Michael, and James Ewinger. "East Ohio Gas Explosions—60 Years Later." *Cleveland Plain Dealer*. October 18, 2004.
"Stricken Suburb Mourns Its Dead in Bitterness Second Day of Tragedy, in Which 164 Children." *Cleveland Plain Dealer*. March 6, 1908.
theenergylibrary.com/node/13077
www.airnews.co.za/march/article_march_the_beguine_story_2.html, www.airnews.co.za, 2010
www.circushistory.org/
www3.gendisasters.com

Discover Thousands of Local History Books
Featuring Millions of Vintage Images

Arcadia Publishing, the leading local history publisher in the United States, is committed to making history accessible and meaningful through publishing books that celebrate and preserve the heritage of America's people and places.

Find more books like this at
www.arcadiapublishing.com

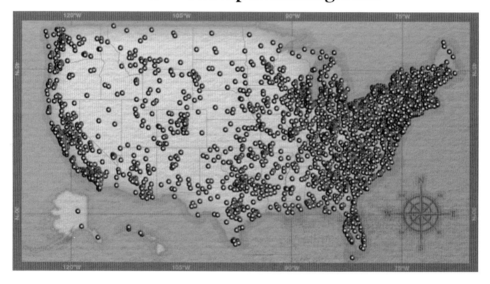

Search for your hometown history, your old stomping grounds, and even your favorite sports team.

Consistent with our mission to preserve history on a local level, this book was printed in South Carolina on American-made paper and manufactured entirely in the United States. Products carrying the accredited Forest Stewardship Council (FSC) label are printed on 100 percent FSC-certified paper.

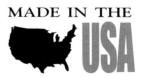